THE
Pink AND Blue
Baby Pages

THE Pink AND Blue Baby Pages

Practical Tips and Advice for New Parents

Laurie Waldstein ♥ Leslie Zinberg

Foreword by Peter S. Waldstein, M.D., F.A.A.P.

CB
CONTEMPORARY
BOOKS
A TRIBUNE NEW MEDIA COMPANY

Library of Congress Cataloging-in-Publication Data

Waldstein, Laurie S.
  The pink and blue baby pages : practical tips and advice for new parents /
Laurie Waldstein, Leslie Zinberg.
      p.   cm.
  Includes index.
  ISBN 0-8092-3396-7
  1. Infants.   2. Infants—Care.   I. Zinberg, Leslie F.   II. Title.
HQ774.W35   1995
649'.122—dc20   95-30763
                                                                       CIP

Cover and interior illustrations by Steve Gillig.

Pronouns alternate gender from chapter to chapter in the interest of fairness.

Notice: The information contained in this book is true and complete to the best of our knowledge. All recommendations are made without any guarantees on the part of the author or of Contemporary Books, Inc. The authors and publisher disclaim all liability in connection with the use of this information.

Published by Contemporary Books, Inc.
Two Prudential Plaza, Chicago, Illinois 60601-6790
Manufactured in the United States of America
International Standard Book Number: 0-8092-3396-7
10   9   8   7   6   5   4   3   2   1

To the men in our lives,
who have helped us realize our dreams . . .

Peter   Michael
Matthew   Steven   Judd   Rodd

We love you!

Contents

Foreword

With the current baby boom exploding throughout this country, my wife, Laurie, and Leslie have written a refreshing parent-to-parent approach to the trials and tribulations of new parenthood. They have carefully prepared and organized practical parenting information, helpful hints, and "mommy remedies" for today's busy parent. Everything has been covered, from setting up a baby's room to easy preparation of baby food to childproofing your home.

I feel this book helps alleviate many of the new parental anxieties most parents possess. Since Laurie and Leslie have children of their own and understand these common fears, they succinctly answer many of the typical day-to-day questions I, and most pediatricians, are frequently asked.

As frustrating as it can be for a pediatrician to receive many unnecessary phone calls, I'm equally concerned about the parents who never call. Patients should always feel they can communicate with their doctor and not be intimidated by asking *any* question. This book takes the pediatrician's directives and advice and explains them in layperson's terms.

I have consulted on this book because I feel there is a tremendous need for a nonmedical, nonpsychological guide that parents can easily refer to. No one has prepared us to become mothers and fathers; parenting is an experience learned through on-the-job training. This reference book is truly a parent's helper and guide.

Peter S. Waldstein, M.D., F.A.A.P.
Clinical Assistant Professor of
Pediatrics, UCLA
Attending Physician, Cedars-Sinai Medical Center
Los Angeles, California

Acknowledgments

Thank you to the people who have always believed in us and
in our undying perseverance . . . in particular, Michael and
Peter. We would like to express our gratitude to
Mark Rosin, who understood our vision and
helped us achieve it. To Tina Kahn, thanks for
sticking with us through the years. And, a
special thank you to Jillian Manus and Nancy
Crossman for making this book a reality.

THE
Pink AND Blue
Baby Pages

Introduction

Those wonderful words "The baby is coming!" are always
closely followed by the sobering question "What do I do
now?" *The Pink and Blue Baby Pages* provides direct, practical,
and simple answers to this question for parents of infants
from birth to twenty-four months. With this book in hand,
you will be able to spend less time worrying about your kids
and more time enjoying them.

We live in a much more mobile society than our
parents did. Often, we live far away from our families, and
those hand-me-down tips that were passed from generation
to generation have to be found elsewhere—such as in this
book.

Parenting can be intimidating and overwhelming. As
parents ourselves, we understand these feelings and concerns. We have created this directory containing everything
we wished we had known when our babies were born. It is
filled with advice and helpful hints that we have accumu-
lated and shared with each other during our children's
formative years.

As mothers, we address the most frequently asked questions facing parents today in a comprehensive, easy to understand manner. The ideas, checklists, and basic preparations detailed in this book will enable you to be more organized and efficient, giving you and your baby more quality time.

The Pink and Blue Baby Pages is a valuable collection of easily accessible information. Whether you have a problem or just a simple question, having this book is like being able to call your mother, sister, or best friend.

Use it in the best of health and happiness.

⊚ 1 ⊚

Before Baby

There are many things you can do to be ready before your baby's auspicious arrival. Three of the most important are choosing a pediatrician, finding help for when you get home from the hospital, and if you need it, selecting day care (see Chapters 2, 3, and 4, "Breast or Bottle?," "Buying for Baby: Comprehensive Checklists," and "Creating Baby's Room"). But don't worry if you haven't gotten it all done before baby gets here—sometimes nature doesn't cooperate! You'll find the following guidelines helpful even if your baby has already arrived.

Choosing a Pediatrician

Remember your favorite schoolteacher, the one you trusted, confided in, and respected? This is the kind of rapport you

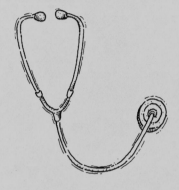

want to establish with your pediatrician. When you're choosing a baby doctor for your newborn, you'll need more than just medical expertise. In the beginning, the pediatrician is unique in that he treats the parents almost as much as the child. Prior to your delivery, it is a good idea to interview at least two pediatricians. Your obstetrician can give you referrals, or you can ask friends and relatives who have children. When you call for an appointment, explain that you would like an "expectant mother's consultation." Here is a list of questions to help you make your choice:

❧ Where is the doctor's office located? Is it convenient for you?

❧ Is the doctor certified by the American Board of Pediatrics? What are his hospital affiliations? Are these hospitals near you?

❧ In an emergency, will the doctor meet you in the middle of the night? At his office? At the hospital? Does the doctor make house calls?

❧ What are the doctor's fees? Are they comparable to those of other doctors in your area?

❧ If you know you're going to have an elective C-section, will the pediatrician along with your obstetrician be present at the birth? What is the fee?

❧ What are the doctor's office hours? Does he have Saturday hours?

❧ How quickly can you see the doctor when your child is sick? Can you call and come in the same day?

❧ Are there specified hours when the doctor answers or returns calls? (As a new parent, you will have many questions. Remember to write them down before calling your pediatrician!)

☀ Is the doctor's nurse or nurse-practitioner available for answering questions? Do you feel comfortable talking to him?

☀ What is the doctor's attitude on breast-feeding vs. bottle-feeding? Is it compatible with yours?

☀ Does the doctor have a partner or associate? Is someone always on call day or night? How often is the doctor on call?

☀ What is the doctor's attitude toward your questions? Is he approachable, forthcoming, and supportive?

☀ Is the doctor's office warm and inviting?

Once you have selected the doctor, call and notify his office.

Finding Help for Mother

When you come home from the hospital, it's a good idea to have someone help you out at home with baby. Birth is a physically and emotionally draining experience. As a new mother, allow yourself the luxury to be babied because those middle-of-the-night feedings catch up with you! With a normal delivery, you'll want someone for at least one week; with a cesarean section, you'll need help for about ten days to two weeks. Assistance can come from a:

☀ Family member

☀ Mother's helper (baby-sitter, college student, family friend, nursing student)

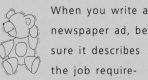
❀ Housekeeper

❀ Baby nurse

Before anyone comes into your home, you, the new mom and dad, should agree on guidelines for the operation of your household. Don't let anyone, even close family members, intimidate you with their babycare philosophies. Listen, but make your own decisions. Here are some pointers to keep in mind when choosing someone to help:

Family Members

❀ Of the family members who can help, with whom do you feel most comfortable?

❀ Is he or she available day or night or both?

❀ For how long can you expect help?

Mother's Helper or Housekeeper

❀ What can you afford?

❀ Are you hiring for a short period of time or will this be a permanent position?

❀ Do you want full-time or part-time assistance?

❀ What responsibilities do you want to delegate to this person?

    ◉ Baby-sitting

    ◉ Cooking for the family

    ◉ Cleaning the house

    ◉ Baby's laundry or family laundry or both

❺ Marketing and running errands

❧ Ask friends and neighbors for referrals, check with the nearest teaching hospital to find out about nursing students, or place an ad in the local newspaper or college daily.

❧ When you interview candidates, make sure they have previous experience taking care of babies and small children.

❧ Personally check out all references.

Baby Nurse

Refer to questions listed under Mother's Helper or Housekeeper, but keep in mind that a baby nurse is primarily for baby! Good resources for finding a nurse can be your pediatrician, obstetrician, Lamaze instructor, and friends who have had babies recently. Interview as many candidates as you feel necessary. Remember to check out recommendations carefully!

A baby nurse's personality should be agreeable and pleasant to all members of the family. If you have older children, it's helpful if the nurse can be attentive and understanding to them, especially when mom is busy with baby. A baby nurse's responsibilities should include the following:

Care of the Baby

❧ Sterilizing and filling baby's bottles if mother is not nursing

❧ Feeding the baby

❧ Doing baby's laundry

❧ Changing baby's sheets

❧ Bathing the baby

❦ Changing diapers

Care of Mom

❦ Cooking for the family

❦ Following nursing mother's diet

❦ Teaching mom babycare techniques or hints

Selecting Day Care

There is nothing more important than the proper care of your baby. If you need to make arrangements for your child in a day care facility, do your homework well! Visit and compare at least two or three day care centers to get an idea of what each offers. Here is a list of questions to consider in choosing the facility:

❦ Is the day care center state accredited?

❦ Are parents welcome to visit any time?

❦ Is the location convenient for you? (Close to home or office or both?)

❦ What are its operating hours? Are early and late hours available? What about holidays? Is the schedule flexible?

❦ How many children are enrolled there?

❦ What is the adult–child ratio? (Find out your state's guidelines for home and other day care facilities.)

❦ What is the turnover rate of caretakers? (If it is unusually high, investigate more thoroughly.)

❦ Are caretakers certified in cardiopulmonary resuscitation (CPR) and first aid?

❧ If your child has an accident, will they contact you first? Is there an emergency facility nearby?

❧ Is English spoken?

❧ Is smoking prohibited on the premises?

❧ Is the center equipped with smoke detectors and fire extinguishers?

❧ What is the facility like?

  ⊚ Is it clean?

  ⊚ Is it childproofed?

  ⊚ Is it homey, warm, and inviting?

  ⊚ How many cribs per room?

  ⊚ How many beds per room?

  ⊚ Where do sick children stay? Do they allow sick children to attend?

  ⊚ Will they dispense medication prescribed for a child?

  ⊚ Is there a fully equipped kitchen? Are meals provided? What kind of meals and snacks do they serve?

❧ Is there a good selection of toys, books, music, and outdoor equipment?

❧ What is the cost? Are there payment options—monthly, weekly, or daily?

Be sure to ask other parents whose children attend the day care center for their evaluations.

෨ 2 ෨

Breast or Bottle?

Whether to breast-feed or bottle-feed is a personal decision. Your baby will spend an important part of each day eating. Therefore, it should be a warm and comfortable experience. When feeding, either breast or bottle, the most important thing is to hold, touch, and talk to your baby.

Breast-Feeding

It's often said that mother's milk is the best. But it's only best if mother is comfortable with breast-feeding. It's crucial not to feel pressured about your decision. There's no right or wrong as long as your child is thriving. If you do breast-feed, the length of time is also a personal choice. Here's some information to help you make up your mind:

PINK AND BLUE HINT

Dad can help occasionally with feedings by giving bottles of expressed breast milk or water.

Advantages of Breast-Feeding

- ❖ Breast milk can help prevent milk allergies. Very few babies are allergic to mom's milk.

- ❖ There is less incidence of colic and other gastrointestinal difficulties.

- ❖ It provides baby with *colostrum* (premilk fluid that comes in before mature milk) which contains many antibodies that protect against bacteria and viruses.

- ❖ It is easier for baby to digest.

- ❖ It builds up baby's immune system.

- ❖ Breast-feeding is more economical.

- ❖ It helps mother's uterus contract faster after the birth.

- ❖ It helps control mother's weight.

- ❖ Medical studies report a lower rate of breast cancer among women who have nursed.

- ❖ It is convenient—there's no need to sterilize or prepare bottles.

Disadvantages of Breast-Feeding

- ❖ Mother *may* experience some discomfort, such as engorged breasts, cracked and bleeding nipples, and leaking.

- ❖ Mother has less free time and less flexibility in her schedule.

- ❖ Dad cannot participate as much with feeding.

- ❖ Both parents may feel uncomfortable not knowing the exact amount of milk consumed by baby at each feeding.

❦ Breast milk digests more quickly, so baby will need to be nursed more frequently.

❦ Breast-fed babies may go on a demand feeding schedule, which means mother has decided to feed the baby as baby demands, or cries for nursing. While a strong emotional bond develops, demand feeding can be rather exhausting.

❦ Some women feel awkward nursing their baby in public.

Time-Tested Advice

If you decide to breast-feed, it can be intimidating simply because you've never done it before. Here are some tips to ease a nursing mother's anxieties.

Preparing for Nursing

❦ In the eighth or ninth month of pregnancy, prepare your nipples by applying lanolin or aloe vera cream. Sit in the sun with exposed breasts for short intervals (use whatever sun block you normally use for the rest of your body). This will keep the skin soft and elastic and toughen the nipples. Hopefully, it will prevent cracked and sore nipples.

❦ Buy at least three well-fitting, comfortable nursing bras at your local maternity shop or department store. Nursing bras are more practical and convenient because you can easily open and close the flap on each breast with one hand (remember baby is being held with the other arm and hand).

❦ Be prepared for leaking milk and the *let-down reflex* (the involuntary hormonal release allowing the muscle to push milk through the lactation system). They are normal and common occurrences. You can purchase nursing pads at the local drugstore. When necessary, insert a pad over each nipple inside the bra. Or cut a thin, flat sanitary napkin in half and use it in the same way.

※ It's helpful to have a few loose-fitting tops for convenience and comfort (sometimes the nipples are tender, and tight clothing can be uncomfortable).

While You're Nursing

PINK AND BLUE HINT

If experiencing back strain while nursing, alleviate the pressure by placing baby on a pillow in your lap. When you raise the pillow, baby will be closer to your breast.

※ While in the hospital, ask nurses to help if you're experiencing any difficulty.

※ Wash your hands and breasts before each feeding; use soap on your hands only and a warm washcloth for your breasts.

※ Hand-express some milk before nursing, if necessary, so the initial fast flow of milk doesn't choke the baby.

※ If baby is having a hard time finding mother's nipple, gently rub the nipple against baby's cheek or lips to help stimulate the *rooting reflex*, an inborn tendency to move toward any pressure on her face.

※ Be sure to allow enough space between breast and baby's nose so she can breathe properly.

※ To break baby's suction from your breast, lift baby's lip by putting your clean finger into the corner of her mouth. Never pull the nipple from baby's mouth, as it can be very painful to your sensitive breasts.

※ Use a bed-rest pillow for back comfort when feeding in bed. It's available at department stores and linen shops.

※ During feedings, take the telephone off the hook or turn on the answering machine.

❧ Be sure to offer both breasts at every feeding and burp baby after each breast.

❧ When you have finished nursing, put a safety pin on the side of the nursing bra that was the last breast used. The side with the pin is the side you will begin nursing on at the next feeding.

❧ When your baby wets six to eight diapers, has two to four bowel movements per day, and has a healthy weight gain, you can be assured your baby is thriving.

❧ The stools of breast-fed babies tend to be mustardy in color, cottage cheesy in consistency, and sometimes look as though they contain seeds.

❧ Be relaxed while nursing; both mom and baby will enjoy the experience more.

What Mom Needs to Know

❧ Drink plenty of fluids because nursing can deplete the liquid in your body. Also, ask your doctor how much milk and other dairy products you should consume.

❧ Eat a well-balanced diet and take doctor-recommended vitamins daily. Foods to avoid:

- Caffeinated products: coffee, tea, colas, chocolate

- Gaseous vegetables: broccoli, cauliflower, cucumber, cabbage, onions, garlic, pickles

- Spicy foods

- Alcoholic beverages

- Dairy products in excess (low-fat and nonfat are healthier choices)

PINK AND BLUE ALERT

Don't fret if your breast-fed baby doesn't have bowel movements regularly. Nursing babies can go up to one week without a bowel movement. Should the baby's belly become distended, call your doctor.

PINK AND BLUE HINT

If you want to express your milk and freeze it, buy a hand-suction breast pump (at the local drugstore) or rent an electric breast pump (ask your doctor or lactation consultant). Mother's milk can be stored in the refrigerator for forty-eight hours or can be frozen in tightly sealed sterile plastic nursing bags for up to six months. Always label the pouch with the date.

PINK AND BLUE HINT

Always keep in mind that whatever mom eats, baby eats. If your child experiences gas or discomfort (drawing up the legs and excessive crying), consider the food you just ate and eliminate it from your diet.

PINK AND BLUE HINT

If mom becomes ill, call the pediatrician and describe your symptoms. The doctor will tell you what is best for baby.

☼ Avoid cigarettes!

☼ For sore nipples, apply a small amount of breast milk to the irritated area and let it air dry.

☼ Don't take any medication without consulting your pediatrician.

☼ Get plenty of rest and go to bed early.

☼ For any questions and additional breast-feeding information, ask your doctor and contact your local La Leche League, breast-feeding support group, or lactation consultant.

If mom and baby no longer enjoy the breast-feeding experience, consider weaning your baby. Your pediatrician will advise you on the formula, bottles, and nipples that are best to use. Don't ever feel a sense of failure if breast-feeding doesn't work out!

Bottle-Feeding

The great thing about bottle-feeding is any responsible member of your family or household can help feed your baby. It's an excellent opportunity for dad to bond with your newborn! Bottle-feeding allows mom's schedule to be more flexible. If you decide to bottle-feed, your pediatrician will recommend the most suitable formula for your baby. If there is a family history of allergies, discuss this with your doctor. It will make a difference in the selection of a formula. Your doctor will also give you instructions on which bottles and nipples to use. Most doctors recommend sterilizing them for at least the first three months of baby's life.

Equipment

If you're going to bottle-feed, here is the equipment you will need:

- Six 8-ounce and four 4-ounce glass or plastic, heat-resistant bottles, with the number of ounces clearly printed on the bottles

- An equal number of nipple collars, disks, and nipple covers

- A dozen or more nipples

- A good bottle and nipple brush

- A funnel

- Tongs (for handling the bottles)

- A punch-type can opener

- A large pot with cover to sterilize bottles, or if you prefer, a sterilizer with a rack

- A small pot with cover to sterilize nipples

- A sterilized container to store nipples, disks, and covers

- A sterilized pitcher and spoon (if using concentrated formula)

- A timer (or use timer on oven)

- Electric bottle warmer (optional)

- A thermos bottle (will keep formula warm or cold for approximately four to five hours; great for the traveling family)

PINK AND BLUE HINT

Buying in bulk
quantity saves
you money!

Formula

Formula is available at grocery stores, drugstores, and large discount stores. It may be purchased in any of the following ways:

❋ Small ready-to-feed bottles (They cost more money but are less time-consuming since there is no preparation or sterilization necessary. Bottles are recyclable.)

❋ 32-ounce cans of ready-to-feed formula which you pour into your own sterilized bottles

❋ Concentrated formula in liquid or powder which must be mixed with boiling water (Carefully follow the exact directions on the can. *Do not improvise!*)

Sterilization

Every doctor has a preferred way to sterilize bottles and bottle accessories. Basically, there are two methods: the dishwasher method and the old-fashioned method. The dishwasher method is just for sterilizing equipment. The old-fashioned method combines preparing concentrated formula and sterilization at the same time. (An alternative, which does not require sterilization, is the plastic nurser with disposable bags. If you choose to use the plastic nursers, follow the directions on the package.) Talk with your doctor before making your choice.

Dishwasher Method:

1. In the sink, thoroughly rinse bottles, bottle covers, collars, disks, nipples, funnel, and tongs in hot water.

2. Place the bottle and funnel on the top shelf of the dishwasher; put collars, covers, and disks in utensil container rack (or for newer models, use covered container).

3. Use the "sani-cycle" cycle of your dishwasher to complete the sterilization process; no soap is necessary.

4. Remove bottles and accessories from the machine with sterilized tongs.

5. For nipples, see sterilization process described below.

Old-Fashioned Preparation Method

1. Wash your hands thoroughly.

2. Wash top of formula can and can opener with hot, soapy water.

3. If you are using concentrated formula or powder, boil the correct amount of water (purified is preferable) three to five minutes; allow to cool in covered pan.

4. Wash all equipment (including bottles, disks, nipple covers, collars, funnel, tongs, and pitcher) in hot, soapy water.

5. If you are using ready-to-feed formula, have supply at hand.

6. To sterilize the bottles, caps, disks, and collars, boil thirty minutes in a sterilizer or large covered pot. If using a rack, place the bottles upside down so steam can get in; sterilize nipples separately in small covered pot—boil in a small amount of water for five minutes.

7. While step 6 is taking place, mix concentrated formula and cooled sterile water in a large sterilized pitcher.

8. When the bottles are ready, fill with appropriate amount per feeding. If using concentrated formula, pour from the pitcher into the bottles. If using ready-to-feed, open

PINK AND BLUE ALERT

Never store left-over ready-to-feed or concentrated formula in an opened can. Discard any remaining contents. Bacteria will form!

PINK AND BLUE ALERT

Mixed formula or already-opened or leftover ready-to-feed bottles may be stored in refrigerator no longer than forty-eight hours.

Time-Tested Advice

♥ When feeding baby, the bottle may be room temperature, slightly warmed (no microwave, please!), or cold from refrigerator. If you're serving the bottle warm, first check the temperature of the formula on your wrist to make sure it's not too hot.

♥ Always test the flow of milk through the nipple before serving baby. If the hole is too large, formula may flow too fast, causing baby to choke or swallow too much air (which can cause gas and stomach discomfort). If the hole is too small, baby will suck in too much air and become frustrated with her feeding.

♥ If there is sufficient space in the refrigerator, store all bottles on one shelf to be sure that all bottles prepared at the same time are used or discarded before feeding from the next batch.

♥ Always hold baby during feeding (never feed baby in infant seat). This is a time for close contact.

♥ If baby doesn't finish all the formula in her bottle, discard the leftover.

cleaned can and pour directly into bottles. Use all contents in the can or discard any remaining formula.

9. Use a sterilized funnel to eliminate spills and waste.

10. After filling bottles, either place the inverted nipple with collar and disk on each bottle or place the nipple upright with collar and cover with cap.

11. Allow bottles to cool a bit before storing in refrigerator.

Your Baby's Bottle-Feeding Stages

Begin feeding baby four ounces of formula. The infant will eat about every three to four hours until she is approximately two months old or eleven to twelve pounds. At two months, the baby should consume about twenty-four ounces of formula per day in four or five feedings. As baby grows, her intake of formula will increase, and she will eat less often.

At four months, with your pediatrician's approval, you can introduce apple, grape, or cranberry juice with "no sugar added" once a day. Dilute the prepared juice by adding an equal amount of water. Once your child has accepted each juice, then any combination may be given in the watered-down form. Orange, grapefruit, and tomato juice should not be introduced until the infant is at least twelve months old, because these juices are highly acidic and can produce an allergic reaction.

At six months, you can begin a regular routine of three feedings a day (eight ounces per feeding), along with the introduction of solid food (see Chapter 11, "Solid Food"). This is a good time to encourage baby to start holding the bottle by herself.

Consult your pediatrician about how long your child should remain on formula. After formula, the recommendation for most children is to drink regular whole milk until age two. At approximately nine months, baby can practice drinking from a cup. Buy a trainer's cup that doesn't tip and has a lid and spout.

Weaning

When weaning your nursing baby, slowly reduce the number of breast-feedings per day. Remember, the more you nurse, the

PINK AND BLUE HINT

Once your baby has mastered holding the bottle alone, a baby bottle straw that attaches inside the bottle to the nipple will make bottle drinking easier for the child. Also, check your stores for the "hands-free" bottle with an extra-long straw and Velcro attachment.

PINK AND BLUE HINT

If baby rejects the bottle from mom (she may still smell and want your milk), have dad or someone else familiar feed the baby her bottle.

PINK AND BLUE HINT

To help reduce engorgement and discomfort, place a cold cabbage leaf, preferably green (purple may stain clothes), over your breasts and under a supportive bra.

more milk your body makes. Therefore, once you're down to one feeding a day, your body will not be producing as much milk. At that time, however, you may still feel engorged. To ease some of the discomfort and pressure in your breasts, express only enough to relieve the pressure. Be sure to wear a supportive bra.

If you prefer the cold turkey, non-reversible weaning method, drink two to three cups of sage tea to drastically reduce your milk production. Sage tea bags can be purchased at your local health food store. To prepare, boil water and let the tea bag steep for two to three minutes. From that point on, temporarily reduce your intake of liquids. Don't be alarmed if your body goes through some hormonal changes, both physically and emotionally. You may even experience flulike symptoms—these are all perfectly normal.

You can start weaning your baby off the bottle at one year. Begin offering the training cup more frequently, filling it with small amounts of formula or juice. If she rejects the cup, don't make an issue of it. Between fifteen and eighteen months, try putting only water in the bottle to encourage cup usage. Prior to bedtime, if your baby still wants her bottle, that's fine. Just remember not to give her the bottle in bed.

ᔆ 3 ᔆ

Buying for Baby: Comprehensive Checklists

Getting ready for baby's arrival is an exciting time, especially in the last few weeks of pregnancy. It can also be very hectic. That's why the more you do ahead of time, the better.

While you're pregnant, make a wish list for all your generous, gift-giving friends and relatives. If someone throws a baby shower for you, be sure to give that person your list. As you receive gifts, cross them off your list so there aren't any duplications. The following lists have been compiled for your convenience. The majority of items may be bought at local discount stores, baby specialty shops, drugstores, and department stores. When making a trip to the store, be sure to carry your list with you. It will be a time saver!

Baby Equipment

Purchasing your baby's equipment is a costly venture, but there are alternatives to buying. Most likely, relatives or friends who have had babies in the past few years will be willing to lend you some of their equipment. Make sure whatever you accept for baby is in excellent condition. The following list contains essential baby equipment. It is cross-referenced for detailed information on specific items. Remember, you will not need all these things immediately.

- Crib and mattress (see Chapter 4, "Creating Baby's Room")

  - Two fitted mattress pads

  - Four to six fitted 100% cotton sheets

  - Three large lap pads

  - Four to six small lap pads

  - Bumpers (no fiberglass inserts)

  - Two crib blankets

- Bassinet or traveling bassinet (see Chapter 4, "Creating Baby's Room"):

  - Two to four fitted bassinet sheets for mattress

  - Blanket

  - Fitted netting (for outdoor use)

  - Bumpers or receiving blankets rolled and placed against sides or both

- Changing table (see Chapter 4, "Creating Baby's Room"):

- Two terry cloth covers for table pad (same size as fitted bassinet sheet)

- Attachable accessory tray (optional)

- Diaper pail with lid

- Diaper hamper (if using cloth diapers)

- Clothes hamper with lid

- Car seat (see Chapters 6 and 12, "Home from the Hospital" and "S.O.S.: Safety Tips"):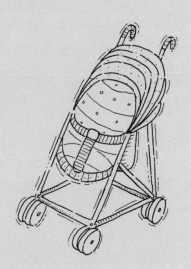

  - Fabric coverlet (optional)

- Infant seat (see Chapter 12, "S.O.S.: Safety Tips"):

  - Fabric coverlet (optional)

- Carriage or stroller or both (see Chapter 12, "S.O.S.: Safety Tips")

- Soft baby carrier for infants

- Baby backpack for babies four months and older

- Playpen and terry cloth cover for pad (see Chapter 12, "S.O.S.: Safety Tips")

- Safety gates (see Chapter 12, "S.O.S.: Safety Tips")

- Portable playpen

- High chair (see Chapter 12, "S.O.S.: Safety Tips")

- Portable baby monitor

- Baby swing (optional)

- Portable changing pad—great for traveling (optional)

Layette: Birth to Six Months

Buying baby clothes is lots of fun, but be careful not to buy everything you see! When purchasing, always consider baby's comfort and your convenience. Don't buy just because the item is cute. Clothes that slip or snap on easily will make dressing your baby less time-consuming (small buttons are no fun to fasten on a wiggling baby). Avoid clothes that require special washing. You want to make your life as simple as possible. Buy clothing large enough to allow room for baby's diaper. It's also best to buy clothes in larger sizes since babies grow so rapidly.

A basic layette for birth to six months should consist of:

- Four to six snap-front tee shirts or wide-neck pullover tee shirts (these cotton wide-neck pullovers are stretchable and slip easily over baby's head)

- Four to six one-piece stretch suits or sleepers (the most practical and comfortable one-piece suits with feet are made of 100% cotton terry cloth or knit and come in summer and winter weights)

- Three sleep gowns or sacques (optional)

- Six bibs

- Three to four soft, washable receiving blankets

- Six cloth diapers (for feeding, burping baby, and protecting the crib sheet when placed under baby's face to catch baby's spit-up)

- Three hooded bath towels and six washcloths

※ Two sweaters or sweatshirts—at least one with a hood (If possible, buy front-opening garments because babies generally dislike over-the-head clothing.)

※ Two hats (a lightweight hat to keep sun off baby's head; a winter-weight hat to protect head and ears from the cold and wind)

※ Three pairs of booties or socks

※ One jacket (appropriate for your local climate)

※ One water-repellent jacket with hood

※ One snowsuit and accessories (for cold weather climate)

※ One baby sleeping bag blanket (optional, see Chapter 14, "Traveling")

※ Diaper bag

PINK AND BLUE HINT

Make sure baby's clothing is flame retardant. Read the labels!

Toiletries

You can go hog-wild buying baby toiletries, but the cost mounts up. A visit to a discount store will be easier on your wallet than purchasing from a retail drugstore. It's best to buy more than one of each item; this will save you numerous trips. You'll soon discover which items you need the most.

※ Disposable diapers (less expensive by the case)

※ Cloth diapers and Velcro diaper covers, or diaper pins and plastic pants (if this is your preference, diaper services are available)

※ Medicated baby powder or cornstarch (if using cornstarch, put it in a shaker)

※ A diaper rash emollient

- Petroleum jelly

- Infant acetaminophen drops (consult your pediatrician)

- Diaper wipes

- Box of tissues

- Sterilized cotton

- Cotton tip applicators

- Alcohol or alcohol pads individually wrapped in foil

- 2" × 2" sterilized gauze pads (to cover circumcised penis and umbilicus)

- Topical antibiotic ointment

- Antiseptic cream

- Hypoallergenic moisturizing cream

- Hydrogen peroxide

- Rectal thermometer or digital ear thermometer

- Infant nasal aspirator

- Saline solution (for nasal aspiration; consult your pediatrician)

- Electrolyte solution (for diarrhea or vomiting; consult your pediatrician)

- Cold mist vaporizer

- Mild hypoallergenic washing detergent

- Hypoallergenic baby soap

- Baby shampoo (a special formula that will not irritate baby's eyes)

- ❦ Baby brush and comb

- ❦ Baby scissors

- ❦ Plastic baby tub (with large bath sponge that fits into baby tub)

- ❦ Small unbreakable jar with lid (for sterilized cotton or gauze pads)

- ❦ Individual room air purifier (optional)

- ❦ Measuring dropper or spoon for administering medicine

- ❦ Hypoallergenic sunscreen

৩ 4 ৩

Creating Baby's Room

When creating your baby's room, there are a few basic principles to keep in mind. The room should be clean, bright, and uncluttered, with good ventilation. Don't be afraid to use color. Color stimulates baby's senses. Keep the room organized and functional, yet fun for baby as she grows older. Avoid dust collectors, like shag carpeting and too many bookshelves. It's easier to maintain a room with a vinyl or wood floor or short pile carpeting. A well-lit room is important, but make sure there's no direct light over the changing table or crib.

Decorating, such as painting and wallpapering, must be done well in advance of baby's arrival. The fumes will linger for at least five days and are too toxic for baby to inhale. In planning baby's room, pay careful attention to the information provided in Chapter 12, "S.O.S.: Safety Tips."

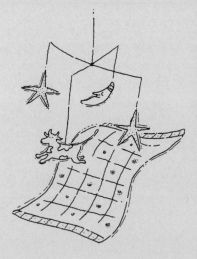

Decorating the Nursery

You have many choices in decorating baby's nursery. Spend some time looking through decorating magazines and catalogues to get ideas. If you're handy and imaginative, you can be creative without spending lots of money, and you'll get a lot of personal satisfaction in the process. Here are a few suggestions to stir those creative juices:

♥ Pick a theme and design the entire room around it. Some examples:

  ◉ Circus

  ◉ Zoo

  ◉ Flowers or gardens

  ◉ Sports

  ◉ Geometric designs

  ◉ Cloud and sky motif

  ◉ Jungle

  ◉ Ballerinas

  ◉ Cartoon characters

  ◉ International themes

  ◉ Aquarium or bird designs

♥ Design a mural. For clever ideas, visit a toy store, school supply house, party shop, or baby furniture store.

♥ Instead of wallpapering the whole room, paint the walls and ceiling and trim the room with a wallpaper border. Borders can be hung along the top of the wall, midwall, or around door and window openings.

☀ Art supply stores have wonderful selections of stencils that can be used on walls, ceilings, and floors. Consult with these stores for the correct type of paint and sealer.

☀ Buy an unfinished chest of drawers, rocking chair, hat rack, or other piece of furniture and decorate it yourself. Use nontoxic paint only!

☀ Select colorful hardware and place on cabinets, doors, or furniture. Make sure there are no sharp or protruding edges, and fasten them securely.

☀ Buy or make a colorful wall hanging, such as a soft sculpture. For ideas, visit a variety of baby stores or fabric or notion outlets. You could also hang a colorful quilt.

Furniture Set-Up

Your baby's crib and changing table are two of the more costly investments you'll make. You may also want to purchase a bassinet and chest of drawers. If family members want to contribute, this is a perfect time!

Bassinet

The bassinet gives baby a secure feeling because it's smaller than a crib. It's terrific for easy mobility around the house, and it's especially convenient for middle-of-the-night feedings. However, it can be used for only approximately six to eight weeks, depending on the size of your baby. Make sure the bassinet you choose has a good mattress. When using it outdoors, cover it with a fitted netting to keep insects away.

To complete the bassinet you will need:

☀ A small lap pad or large folded pad (placed over the mattress)

❦ A bassinet-sized fitted sheet (placed over the lap pad). Save this sheet because it can also be used as a cover for the changing table pad.

❦ Bumpers or receiving blankets rolled up and placed against the sides

❦ Receiving blanket or top sheet or both (optional)

❦ Small blanket

An alternative to the bassinet is a baby basket, which can also be used for traveling. It should be used only for the first six weeks. Never use the basket as a car seat. Always remember to support the bottom of the basket when carrying baby.

Crib

A crib and mattress are important investments. This is not the place to cut corners. The crib must meet today's safety standards set by the Consumer Product Safety Commission (look for the label). These safety standards include the following guidelines:

❦ All paint must be lead free

❦ Guard rails should be covered with nontoxic plastic

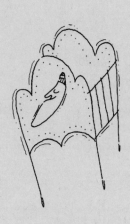

❦ All edges and corners must be smooth and rounded (no splinters, cracks, or protruding points)

❦ Rail bars should be no more than 2⅜″ apart

❦ Mattress must fit exactly into crib (no extra spaces)

❦ Mattress should be firm

PINK AND BLUE ALERT

Carefully follow crib assembly directions supplied by the manufacturer. Variations (with screws, nuts, and bolts left over) are not safe.

Time-Tested Advice

❧ Rotate mattress every few months.

❧ Wipe the crib periodically with a clean damp cloth (as baby gets older, she will become more oral and explore everything with her mouth).

❧ Bumpers are a must; they should fit snugly around the edge of the crib and have at least six ties or snaps (trim down long ties to avoid entanglement).

❧ Avoid bumpers with fiberglass inserts; they're highly flammable.

❧ Side rails must always be locked and secured after baby is in crib. It never hurts to recheck!

❧ Crib should be positioned on an inside wall. Avoid placement near a window with dangling cords or in direct line of heat or air-conditioning vent.

❧ To complete the crib you will need:

  ⊚ A fitted mattress pad

  ⊚ Large lap pad (placed over mattress pad)

  ⊚ Fitted 100% cotton sheets (easy to wash, no ironing)

  ⊚ Smaller-sized lap pad (placed over sheet in area baby sleeps in)

  ⊚ Top flat sheet (optional)

  ⊚ Blanket

❧ Do not use a pillow because of danger of suffocation.

PINK AND BLUE HINT

Don't forget to wash new clothing or linens before using them for the first time. It's also a good idea to wipe down new plastic toys.

♥ Crib sheets should always be clean and fresh. Change sheets as often as necessary.

♥ Optional crib accessories include:

  ◎ A mobile (do not place directly over baby's head)

  ◎ Stuffed animals or toys (Watch out for buttons, wind-up keys, long strings, and protruding parts. Don't crowd crib with too many things.)

Changing Table

A well-organized changing table is the key to easy, safe diapering and dressing. If all the items are at your fingertips, there will be no need to leave baby alone. Remember, your baby can roll off the tabletop in a split second! Always keep one hand firmly gripped on baby's body, especially when reaching to a bottom shelf or drawer. If you have forgotten something or the phone or doorbell rings, take baby with you. Items to keep immediately available at the changing table are:

❀ Diapers

❀ Alcohol (or alcohol pads individually wrapped in foil)

❀ Sterilized cotton

❀ Jar with gauze pads prepared with topical antibiotic ointment or cream (for circumcised penis)

❀ Medicated baby powder or cornstarch in a shaker

❀ A diaper rash emollient

❀ Diaper wipes

❀ Petroleum jelly

❀ Hypoallergenic moisturizing cream

- ❧ Cotton tip applicators

- ❧ Baby nose aspirator

- ❧ Baby scissors and soft nail file

- ❧ Baby brush and comb

- ❧ Box of tissues

If there are other children in your house, it's safer to put these items on a high shelf—out of children's reach, but easily accessible to an adult. Be sure this shelf is not directly over the changing table. You don't want anything to fall on baby!

Top of Changing Table

- ❧ A terry cloth cover over vinyl changing pad

- ❧ Lap pad over terry cover (to save washing time)

- ❧ Reusable cotton bassinet sheets (when terry cloth cover is soiled)

Middle Shelf

- ❧ Diapers—disposable or cloth (If using cloth, then keep the necessary accessories here. See Chapter 9, "Personal Baby Care," for diapering accessories.)

- ❧ Baby toiletries (if there are no small children in the house)

- ❧ Layette items such as undershirts, one-piece suits or pajamas, quick-change clothing, and socks or booties

Bottom Shelf

- ❧ Crib and bassinet sheets

- ❧ Lap pads
- ❧ Receiving blankets
- ❧ Cloth diapers (for burping and spit-up)
- ❧ Hooded towels and washcloths

Nursery Accessories

Now you're almost done with baby's nursery. The finishing touches can be completed at your convenience. Some accessories are more important than others.

Here's the final checklist (in order of importance) for baby's arrival:

- ❧ Diaper pail with lid and lock (look for pail with built-in deodorizer compartment)
- ❧ Diaper hamper with lid (if using cloth diapers)
- ❧ Clothes hamper with lid
- ❧ A night light with adjustable brightness
- ❧ A portable baby monitor or intercom
- ❧ A clock
- ❧ Rocking chair or comfortable chair for an adult
- ❧ A chest of drawers (optional, more necessary as baby gets older)
- ❧ A twin bed or sofa (optional)

๑ 5 ๑

Delivery

By the end of the ninth month, you probably feel as if you're
more than ready to deliver. You've chosen your pediatrician
(hopefully), found help for your return home, and checked
and rechecked your checklists. Now there's just one thing
missing—baby!

Getting Ready for the Hospital

Your "birthing bag" and personal suitcase
should be prepared in advance, since you
never know when baby will really arrive!
Along with these, keep a heavy large plastic
trash bag to sit on in the car on your way to the hospital.
This will protect car upholstery in case your water breaks.
Here are the items you'll want to pack:

❀ A "birthing bag" with everything you will need during labor and delivery:

   ⊙ Admission forms and insurance card

   ⊙ A personal item to be used as a focal point during intense labor

    ⊙ A book, magazine, or playing cards for early labor

     ⊙ Music—tape recorder or compact disc recorder with tapes and discs

      ⊙ Lip gloss for dry mouth

      ⊙ Electrolyte drink (if permitted)

      ⊙ Snacks for dad or labor assistant

     ⊙ Extra pillows

    ⊙ Socks (to keep mom's feet warm)

   ⊙ Cold pack and hot-water bottle

   ⊙ Breath freshener that doesn't nauseate mom

   ⊙ Tennis balls for counterpressure with back labor

   ⊙ Oil, lotion, or powder for massage

   ⊙ Camera and film

   ⊙ Video recorder with videocassette

❀ Your personal suitcase filled with necessities for your hospital stay:

   ⊙ Two or three nightgowns or nightshirts (if nursing, make sure there's a front opening so breast-feeding is convenient)

   ⊙ Bathrobe

- Slippers
- Nursing bras and pads (if nursing)
- Two or three pairs of underwear
- Toothbrush and toothpaste
- Shampoo, brush, and comb (hair dryer optional)
- Deodorant
- Powder
- Makeup
- Something comfortable to wear home from the hospital
- An outfit and receiving blanket for baby's trip home
- Plenty of coins for dad's numerous phone calls
- Your address book with phone numbers

If you know you're having a cesarean section, be prepared for a longer hospital stay.

In the Hospital

While you are in the hospital, rest and pamper yourself. It's a good idea to get out of bed and walk around as soon as possible. Take advantage of any classes or special television programs available through the hospital. If the hospital has a rooming-in policy, where baby stays in the room with you, try it. This will give mom and dad the opportunity for hands-on experience, while still having the support and advice of the hospital staff nearby.

PINK AND BLUE ALERT

Don't be surprised if your health insurance carrier allows only a twenty-four hour stay for a normal vaginal delivery.

Obstetrician and Pediatrician Hospital Visits

When your obstetrician visits you, don't hesitate to ask him any questions you may have about the changes your body is experiencing. Many women feel a certain "low" often referred to as *postpartum blues*. This emotion is common to many new mothers and will pass. If this happens to you, schedule a postpartum office visit to discuss your feelings.

Your pediatrician will be examining your newborn baby within the first twenty-four hours of life. When he visits you, he will tell you all the relevant information you need and want to know. Most doctors provide new parents with a baby pamphlet that highlights immediate daily infant care. In order to make the best use of his visit, write down your inquiries and observations so you are prepared when he arrives. Suggested questions are:

※ When is the first office visit scheduled?

※ How do you care for the umbilicus? If you have a son, are there special directions for the circumcision?

※ If you're breast-feeding, what are his suggested guidelines?

※ If you're bottle-feeding, what is his formula preference?

※ Does he have a particular time when he takes calls?

Siblings and Other Visitors

Maternity visiting hours are generally shorter than standard hospital visiting hours. Check these times prior to your anticipated delivery due date so friends and family can plan a visit, should you desire company. If you are not feeling up to it, don't be afraid to say no to visitors. Insist that visitors not feeling well delay their visit until they are completely healthy.

If there are siblings at home, find out the hospital's visitation policy for children. It is extremely important that your older children see you and be reassured that everything is okay. To avoid resentment and sibling rivalry, make sure you include the older children as soon as possible. Here are some suggestions to ease a sibling's first visit with the new baby:

- If the hospital permits direct contact with baby, then let your child participate by holding or touching him.

- Whoever brings your child to the hospital (preferably daddy, grandparents, or close family relations) should be the same person who takes him home. Before coming to the hospital, it's a good idea to have this person explain the hospital's rules.

- Plan to have no other visitors when your child arrives. He needs to know this is a special visit just for him.

- Mom should keep in close telephone contact with baby's siblings until her return home. Send handwritten notes home to them with dad.

- Prepare your child for the reality that in the first few months of life, baby will not be as much fun as he expects.

- Keep siblings' schedules as routine as possible (consistency reinforces security).

- Encourage your child to draw a picture or make something for mom and baby.

Verifying Baby's Birth Certificate

Be sure the hospital has all the correct information for baby's birth certificate. While you're in the hospital, you'll be asked to fill out a form. The hospital will forward this form to the county, and you'll receive an official certificate approximately three months later.

೧ 6 ೧

Home from the Hospital

For the last nine months, you've only imagined what it would be like to come home with your new bundle of joy. Now the day is here, and you're filled with emotions of love, excitement, and apprehension. The first order of business is to transport baby home safely.

Baby Car Seat

You must have a car seat properly installed in your car for baby's ride home from the hospital. Even if it's a short trip around the block, baby must always be secured in the car seat. Most accidents occur within a two-mile radius of home. Car safety restraints should be a non-negotiable policy within your household. There are *no* exceptions!

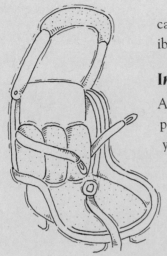

Infants up to twenty pounds must be placed in rear-facing car seats. Your two choices are an infant car seat or a convertible car seat.

Infant Car Seat

An infant car seat is only for babies weighing up to twenty pounds. Some infant car seats also double as infant carriers. If you buy this kind of car seat, you will not need a standard infant seat. However, once baby reaches the maximum weight of twenty pounds, you will need to purchase a convertible car seat. Baby's head should be supported with an infant headrest or propped up with jelly-rolled receiving blankets.

Convertible Car Seat

This type of car seat can be used from birth to forty pounds. When used for an infant, it can be positioned to hold baby at an angle similar to the infant car seat, supporting baby in a rear-facing position. As baby grows, the seat can be adjusted gradually to a more upright position to accommodate baby's height and weight. While this car seat is heavier and more cumbersome than an infant car seat, you won't have to purchase two different car seats. However, this seat cannot be utilized as a portable infant seat.

Whichever car seat or seats you select, remember to follow the manufacturer's instructions carefully. If you use the car seat improperly, it will *not* protect your child. Be sure to buy or use car seats manufactured after January 1, 1981, when new federal safety standards were established. While the safest location for baby's car seat is in the center of the back seat, most parents of newborns prefer to place baby in the front passenger seat because it's reassuring to be near one another. But, if your car has a passenger-side air bag, *don't* put a rear-facing car seat in front of the bag. Place baby in the back seat (rear-faced position) and buy a special safety mirror so you can always keep an eye on baby. (For more detailed car seat information, see Chapter 12, "S.O.S.: Safety Tips.")

Balancing Siblings, Pets, and Company

When you first come home from the hospital, it's a bit overwhelming. Your top priority is to balance the many facets of your new family life. Remember, you also need to reserve and preserve your energy. When baby rests, mom should rest.

Siblings

To encourage good relations between the new baby and siblings:

♥ When mom and baby first come home, let the older brothers and sisters sit in a chair and hold the new baby. Don't forget to take pictures!

♥ Remember to include siblings in simple tasks to help you care for baby. Let siblings enjoy their new important role.

♥ Give big brothers and sisters the extra special love and attention they need at this time. Take them out to dinner, a movie, or a special event.

♥ Allow quality time alone with each sibling so he or she doesn't feel forgotten.

♥ Have about a half-dozen wrapped gifts ready for each sibling. These gifts will come in handy when visitors arrive with presents for baby only. They will help your older child feel included. These gifts do not have to be elaborate or expensive. Examples for younger children are:

⊚ Coloring books and crayons

⊚ Paint-with-water books and paint brush

PINK AND BLUE HINT

A nice way to begin a sibling's acceptance of baby is to give a specially wrapped gift from baby to brother or sister.

- Play dough or clay (lots of fun with cookie cutters)

- Puzzles

- Books

- A new doll or stuffed animal

- Building blocks

- A cassette, CD, or record

- A video cassette

- Baking sets (they come packaged with small cake pans, plastic cookie cutters, and cake and cookie mix)

- Activity books

- Art supplies (construction paper, finger paint, water colors)

- A ball

Examples for older children are:

- Stickers and sticker book

- Stamp collecting or coin collecting albums (a great time to start a project together)

- An inexpensive camera with a few rolls of film (make a scrapbook)

- A model toy kit

- A puzzle

- Any arts and crafts project

- A cassette, CD, or record

- An electronic video game or computer game

- Books

- Modeling clay

- Flower or vegetable seeds to plant a garden with their own gardening tools

- A cookbook and ingredients for one or two recipes

- Any sports-related item (soccer ball, basketball, football, jump rope)

- Additions to an already established hobby or interest

Pets

A pet cannot be held accountable for its behavior. Even if the pet has been in your family for a long time, don't take chances. Pets get jealous, too! For health's sake, a visit to your veterinarian is important, since pets can carry diseases. Make sure your pet has no worms and is current with all immunizations.

Some suggestions for introducing baby and pet are:

- Let your dog sniff baby's foot so it can distinguish baby's scent and become familiar and protective.

- If you have a cat and it's not declawed, be careful.

- If you own a bird, keep it in a cage in a room that baby will not occupy.

- Give your pet lots of special attention.

PINK AND BLUE ALERT
Don't flea bomb your home while you are pregnant or in the first few months of baby's life.

PINK AND BLUE ALERT
Never leave baby and your pet alone together! A pet's behavior can be unpredictable.

Company

Family members and friends will all want to come and visit you right away. Select times that are convenient for you to receive guests. Make sure you don't have too many people over at one time. And, if you're not up to having visitors, don't be embarrassed to say so.

It's OK for everyone to speak in normal tones. Your baby needs to learn to get used to different noise levels. Keeping your household too quiet will not be beneficial in the long run. Your baby needs to adapt to *your* lifestyle. Here are some rules to follow with company:

1. Absolutely no smoking around the baby.

2. All visitors must be healthy. If it makes you feel more comfortable, have your guests wear sterile, disposable face masks (available at the hospital or drugstore).

3. Young children should avoid close contact with your newborn for the first month.

4. No one should kiss baby's lips.

5. Let people know when you're tired.

Circumcision and Umbilicus

There are two immediate physical needs that must be taken care of when baby comes home from the hospital. They are the umbilicus and, if you have chosen to do so, circumcision.

Circumcision

If you have had your son circumcised, keep his penis covered with a gauze pad and topical antibiotic ointment the first day after the procedure. Fresh ointment and gauze must be applied each time you change baby's diaper. After the second day, apply the ointment directly onto the circumcision until it heals. If any inflammation or bleeding occurs, call your doctor.

Umbilicus (Bellybutton)

Be sure to clean the cord three to four times a day until it falls off. This usually occurs between two to four weeks after birth. To take proper care of the umbilical cord:

☀ Gently dab the prepackaged alcohol pads or sterilized cotton dipped in alcohol on and around the cord. Continue doing this for a few days after the cord has fallen off.

☀ Keep the diaper from rubbing against the umbilical by diapering below the bellybutton.

☀ Keep the cord exposed and open to air as much as possible. This will promote quick healing.

☀ Don't bathe baby until the cord falls off. Until then, just carefully sponge bathe.

☀ If any oozing, inflammation, or foul odor occurs, call your pediatrician.

ʘ 7 ʘ

How to Handle Burping,
Colic, and Crying

There are certain stages in your baby's growth and development that you'll learn to cope with. Getting to know your baby's needs and personality will take time. He is going to express himself in many ways and react to your responses accordingly. Burping, colic, and crying are usually the by-products of one culprit—gas. As new parents, the more you know about these three things, the easier they are to respond to in caring for your baby.

Burping

When baby sucks on a nipple (breast or bottle), he is bound to swallow unwanted air that can cause belly discomfort.

PINK AND BLUE HINT

When burping baby, drape a clean cloth diaper over your shoulder or lap to keep yourself clean.

Burping helps alleviate this discomfort. It also gives baby a chance to stop and digest what he has just consumed. Always burp your baby as you switch him from one breast to the other, or every few ounces when bottle-feeding. Some newborns don't burp readily, so be patient and don't pat their backs too hard or for too long. A little spit-up is not unusual, even hours after feeding, but if your baby spits up constantly and the quantity is excessive, call your pediatrician.

Burping Techniques

Three techniques are most often used. Try them all and see which one works best for baby.

1. **Over the shoulder:** Firmly hold baby against your shoulder, supporting the baby's back with one hand and patting or rubbing the back with your other hand.

2. **Upright sitting position:** Hold baby on your lap in an upright position, head leaning forward, chest supported by your arm. Make sure baby's head and neck are carefully supported. Rub or pat his back.

3. **Lap position:** Place your baby's face sideways on your lap with his head resting comfortably on one leg. Hold baby securely with one hand and rub or pat baby's back with the other.

As your baby grows older, his need to be burped will diminish.

Colic

Colic is one of the great mysteries of the medical world. There are many theories about it but no concrete evidence to support them. Colic is definitely not the result of bad parenting. Colic is not a disease, but a condition that manifests itself as fretfulness, lengthy periods of crying, loud screams after being fed, and abdominal cramping (drawing the knees up, wildly flexing and extending the legs). There can be inconsolable bouts lasting as long as two to three hours. A colicky baby is *not* an unhealthy baby. Colic usually begins in the second or third week of life and resolves itself by age three months. During this time, it's helpful to have someone who can relieve you of your parental duties for a few hours in order to save your sanity.

Time-Tested Advice

* To lessen gas for bottle-fed babies, be sure to burp thoroughly every few ounces; for breast-fed babies, burp after each breast has been emptied.

* Hold baby face down, supporting head and neck with your hand. Allow the abdomen to rest on your knees and very gently move knees in a circular motion. At the same time, stroke or rub baby's back.

* Fill a tightly sealed hot water bottle with warm water and cover it with a soft towel or clean cloth diaper. Lay the baby face down with his tummy resting on the bottle.

* If baby is breast-fed, review the foods you have eaten in the last twenty-four to seventy-two hours. Eliminate caffeine (coffee, tea, cola, or chocolate), gaseous vegetables (onion, garlic, broccoli), and spicy foods, or cut down on fruits and dairy products.

❤ Your baby's formula may be the culprit. Consult your pediatrician because you may have to make a change.

❤ Try bottle-feeding baby weakened herbal chamomile tea with a pinch of sugar; it may help relax his tummy.

❤ Remain calm. Try not to become too tense, although it is an extremely anxious feeling not being able to console your hurting baby.

❤ Colicky babies are sometimes comforted by motion. The following are motion remedies (try any or all until you find one that works):

   ෂ Rock baby in a rocking chair

   ෂ Place baby in stroller and walk

   ෂ Drive around the block with baby in car seat (you may be spending more time in your car than in your house, but if it works, go with it)

   ෂ Walk baby while applying gentle but firm pressure to the abdomen (if there are other adults at home, take turns)

❤ Try an anti-gas, anti-flatulent remedy (simethicone drops). They're available over-the-counter; however, do *not* administer without consulting your pediatrician first.

Crying

Your baby's only way of communicating is through crying. Therefore, you will learn (with time and patience) to differentiate the various cries your baby makes. Up until the age of three months, you should pick up your baby and comfort and cuddle him when he cries. You *cannot* spoil a newborn—he needs to feel secure in his new environment.

Clues to Crying

When your baby cries, it's usually for one or more of the following reasons:

- Hunger
- Dirty diaper
- Fatigue
- Colic
- Gas
- Attention (usually in babies three months and older)
- Teething (usually begins after three months)

Every baby tends to have a fussy period. This is perfectly normal. It usually occurs around the dinner hour when dad comes home from work, siblings return from school, and mom has her attention focused on dinner and settling down the household. Some babies are just fussier than others because of their personalities.

Time-Tested Advice

- In contrast with the usual reasons your baby cries, it's easy to recognize a cry of pain, because this cry tends to be loud and piercing.

PINK AND BLUE HINT

If baby is particularly fussy, and you know everything is all right, try a gentle body massage (including the feet). It may relax baby.

♥ When you've ruled out the typical reasons your baby cries and he is experiencing prolonged bouts of inconsolable sobs, call your doctor.

♥ After your baby is three months old, don't fall into the trap of always running to him and holding him every time he cries. If you pick him up and the crying stops immediately, then your baby is smarter than you—and the manipulation has begun! Don't reinforce this bad habit or it will come back to haunt you. Just pick up baby as needed. Your parental instincts will guide you.

♥ Many babies can be soothed and comforted when crying by sucking on a pacifier. If you object to a pacifier and your child still fusses, you can try to teach baby to find his fist or thumb to suck on. Sucking is a natural instinct for babies and shouldn't be suppressed (see Chapter 10, "Sleep"). However, if your child is not interested in sucking on a pacifier, his thumb, or fist, you should not force him to do so.

♥ Motion remedies that can be useful to soothe crying are listed in the advice on colic on page 54.

ා 8 ා

Medical and Dental Baby Care

When it comes to caring for your baby's health and welfare, keep in mind the old adage "an ounce of prevention is worth a pound of cure." An important part of this care is surrounding yourself with professionals who make you and your baby feel comfortable and secure. The one person whose telephone number should be inscribed in your memory is your pediatrician.

Monthly Visits to the Pediatrician

Your first visit to the pediatrician will generally be two weeks after baby's birth. In a normal, full-term baby, birth weight usually decreases approximately 10% during the first week.

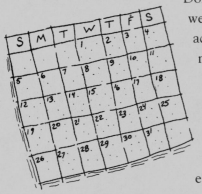

Don't be alarmed because baby should regain that birth weight within about two weeks. At your first office visit, in addition to the routine examination, the doctor will measure your baby's head circumference.

You and your infant will visit the pediatrician once a month for the first year. These monthly checkups will monitor baby's growth and development, nutrition, and socialization. After her first birthday, the pediatrician should see your child every three months—at fifteen, eighteen, twenty-one, and twenty-four months. When you come in for your monthly visits, bring along written questions or comments about your baby's progress and development. This will help you avoid unnecessary phone calls to your doctor later. At monthly checkups, your baby's basic physical exam will include:

- Height and weight

- Head (fontanelle)

- Ears, eyes, nose, and throat

- Listening to baby's heart and lungs

- Palpation of abdomen

- Genitalia (in a boy, descended testicles)

- Flexing and rotating of hips and feet

Each month of your baby's life will bring new and exciting developments. It is extremely important to make the monthly visits to the doctor so your baby can receive vital immunizations and routine examinations. Preventive medicine promotes healthy lives!

The following is a month-by-month overview of immunizations and developmental milestones. Remember, these milestones are just guidelines. Every child develops differently.

One Month

- Hepatitis B immunization

- Head circumference measurement

- Visual tracking (vision is unclear at this stage)

- Begins lifting head (when sleeping, can turn head from side to side)

Two Months

- DPT (Diphtheria, Pertussis, Tetanus)

- OPV (Oral Polio Vaccine)

- HIB (Haemophilus Influenza Type B—Meningitis prevention and other "H" flu diseases)

- Examination of skin for color, tone, rashes, and lesions

- Social smile

- Follows objects with eyes

- Lifts head with better control

- Makes "cooing" sounds

Three Months

- Hepatitis B immunization

- Head circumference measurement

- Lifts head easily

- Baby starts turning over, first from belly to back, then back to belly

- "Coos" and squeals

PINK AND BLUE ALERT

There is a new shot available called Tetramune, which combines the DPT and HIB into one vaccine. Check with your pediatrician.

- Drools

- Hand-in-the-mouth routine

- Begins fascination of seeing reflection in mirror

Four Months

- DPT

- OPV

- HIB

- Laughs

Five Months

- No immunizations this month

- Baby easily turns over, first from belly to back, then back to belly

- Reaches or grasps objects and brings them to mouth

Six Months

- DPT

- OPV

- HIB

- Head circumference measurement

- Sits up unassisted

Seven Months

- No immunizations this month

❦ Begins creeping movement which leads to crawling

❦ Starts to respond to simple games like patty cake and peek-a-boo

Eight Months

❦ No immunizations this month

❦ Crawls

❦ Makes more sounds

❦ Begins to pull up to a stand while holding on

❦ Can grasp a ball

❦ May develop a fear of strangers

Nine Months

❦ Hepatitis B immunization

❦ Head circumference measurement

❦ Continues pulling up to a standing position

❦ Will attempt walking while holding on (called *cruising*)

❦ Can go from lying on stomach to sitting up to standing up

Ten Months

❦ No immunizations this month

❦ Cruises

❦ Says "mama" and "dada"

❦ Waves bye-bye

- Fine motor skills more fully developed (picks up simple objects with hands)

Eleven Months

- No immunizations this month
- Gains more confidence cruising
- Stands alone for short periods of time

Twelve Months

- MMR vaccine (Measles, Mumps, and Rubella)
- TB test (Tuberculosis)
- Varicella vaccine (Chicken pox)—optional, but highly recommended
- Head circumference measurement
- Begins walking alone
- Can begin cup training
- Fine motor skills more defined

Fifteen Months

- HIB vaccine
- Follows simple commands
- May name familiar objects
- Feeds herself finger foods
- Uses bottle less frequently
- More proficient drinking out of a cup

❦ Begins to comprehend the meaning of *no*

Eighteen Months

❦ DPT

❦ OPV

❦ Vocabulary expanding

❦ Improved dexterity with hands and fingers

❦ Begins to run (stiffly)

❦ Recognizes wet and dirty diapers

Twenty-One Months

❦ No immunizations this month

❦ Follows simple directions and commands

❦ Begins to use spoon independently

❦ Weaning off bottle

❦ Runs with more confidence

Twenty-Four Months

❦ TB skin test

❦ Runs well

❦ Goes up and down stairs

❦ Climbs (beware!)

❦ Two- to three-word fluency—strings two to three words together

❦ Understands the word *no*

PINK AND BLUE HINT

When babies begin to walk, it's better for them to walk barefoot. Gripping the floor with no shoes on builds confidence. Walking in socks can easily make a baby slip and fall.

☀ Can listen to short stories with pictures

☀ Handles spoon and cup well

☀ Fine motor coordination better developed

☀ Begins to interact socially with other children

Some children progress faster than others. As a parent, it's natural to be concerned about the developmental steps your child will take, but don't compare one child's growth and development with another's. You are raising an individual. If you have any questions or anxieties, be sure to discuss them with your pediatrician.

Phone Calls to the Pediatrician

Nobody knows your baby better than you do. There will be times your parental instincts tell you something is just not right. For a new parent, the first time baby gets sick can be frightening. Stay calm and focused. Baby can pick up on your nervous "vibes"!

These symptoms warrant a call to your doctor:

☀ Fever

☀ Diarrhea or constipation

☀ Runny nose (yellowish-green)

☀ Coughing

☀ Labored breathing

☀ Tugging on ear

☀ Glassy eyes

☀ Vomiting

☀ Inconsolable crying or whining

♥ Excessive clinging

♥ Change in sleeping patterns

♥ Loss of appetite

♥ Listlessness

♥ Skin rash or discoloration

♥ Unusual bleeding

Don't be afraid to call the doctor when you're concerned, whether it's during the day or middle of the night. Always have paper and pen nearby and be prepared with the following information:

♥ Baby's age

♥ Baby's weight

♥ Temperature

♥ Symptoms (when they began and how long the condition has persisted)

♥ Pharmacy telephone number

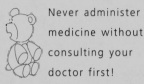

PINK AND BLUE ALERT

Never administer medicine without consulting your doctor first!

Teething and Dental Hygiene

All babies teethe. For some babies it's a cakewalk; for others, it's a painful journey. Teething can begin as early as three months, but as with every aspect of children's development and growth, there is no exact time line.

Usually, the lower front central incisors are the first two teeth to emerge. Teething is not a constant or chronic condition; it's sporadic. Your baby may experience discomfort which can manifest itself in many ways. When in doubt about whether your baby is reacting to teething, your best resource

PINK AND BLUE HINT

To protect clothing from drool, have baby wear a bib.

PINK AND BLUE ALERT

Never put your baby to bed with a bottle! If a child is allowed to suck on a bottle for an extended period, natural sugars in formula and unsweetened juices can cause enamel erosion (bottle teeth).

PINK AND BLUE ALERT

Baby should be sitting in an upright position and never left alone when munching on teething foods.

is your pediatrician. She can help you differentiate between teething symptoms and a real illness. Here are typical teething symptoms:

- Loose stools
- Clear mucus from runny nose
- Excessive drooling
- Low-grade fever
- Loss of appetite
- Skin rash (usually on the face and bottom)
- Restless sleep (day or night)
- Cranky and irritable behavior
- Tugging on the ear (If this persists, call your pediatrician; baby may have an ear infection.)
- Putting any object into mouth

Time-Tested Advice

While there are no cures for teething, here are some time-tested teething aids that may ease baby's pain:

- Frozen bagel with no seeds
- Fat, raw, cold carrot (only for a baby with very few teeth because carrot bits can cause choking)
- Frozen teething ring or teething toy
- Small frozen washcloth (wet washcloth and place in freezer overnight)

💗 Over-the-counter topical anesthetic or numbing gel (first consult your pediatrician)

💗 Your clean finger

Baby teeth need proper cleaning to prevent decay and mouth odor. Each day at bath time, wipe the gums and teeth with a soft, damp washcloth or gauze wrapped around your finger. The good dental hygiene you are practicing for your child is good preparation for the later years. By the time your child is two-and-a-half years old, twenty primary teeth should have appeared.

A well-balanced, low-sugar diet is also important. Your pediatrician will advise whether or not fluoride supplements are needed in your area. The average age for baby's first dental visit is two-and-a-half to three years old. Consult your pediatrician for recommendations.

Your Home Medicine Cabinet

It's a good idea to keep your medicine cabinet fully equipped. All medications must be kept out of a child's reach. Once again, do *not* administer medicine without first consulting your pediatrician. Here are the items you will need:

💥 Digital ear thermometer (inserted in the ear to measure temperature) or rectal thermometer (apply petroleum jelly to the tip prior to inserting in rectum; always clean with alcohol after use)

💥 Rubbing alcohol

💥 Hydrogen peroxide

💥 Acetaminophen drops

PINK AND BLUE HINT

Take an infant CPR (cardiopulmonary resuscitation) and first aid class. To locate a class, check with your doctor, local YMCA, or Red Cross.

- Electrolyte solution (available in fruit flavor)
- Topical antibiotic ointment
- Syrup of ipecac
- Antidiarrheal/antispasmodic over-the-counter liquid medicines
- Nasal syringe
- Saline nasal spray
- Bandages
- Gauze pads
- Adhesive tape
- Instant ice packs
- Droppers and child's special measuring spoon or cup
- Cold air humidifier
- Hot water bottle or heating pad (use at warm temperatures)
- First aid book and kit
- Small flashlight

ම9ම

Personal Baby Care

Your baby's personal hygiene is part of a daily routine. Diapering, bathing, and dressing require organization and quick hands. They will become more fun for you as you become more adept. If you find a technique that works well for you and baby, go with it. Nothing is written in stone. Improvise to suit baby's needs.

Bath Time

Bath time should be a fun and relaxing experience for parent and baby. But don't be surprised if baby cries and flails his arms and legs the first few times you attempt bathing; it's a new and frightening sensation. To calm him, play some peaceful music. While baby won't be down in the trenches,

PINK AND BLUE ALERT

It is not advisable to give your child bubble baths. While they are fun, they can cause urinary tract infections in girls and urethritis in boys.

69

digging and getting dirty, a daily bath or at least sponge bath is a good idea.

Sponge Bath

Until the umbilical cord falls off or circumcision heals, a sponge bath is recommended. Remember to have all your bath items available within hand's reach. These include:

- Two wet, warm washcloths

- A hooded towel

- Baby soap

- Baby powder

- Rash ointment (if needed)

- Alcohol pads or sterile cotton and alcohol

- Gauze pads with topical antibiotic ointment

- Cotton tip applicators

- A clean diaper

- Clothing

To sponge-bathe baby:

1. Choose a room that has either a changing table or bed, or, if you choose the bathroom, pad the floor or counter with a soft towel.

2. Be sure the room is warm.

3. Lay a lap pad under baby.

4. Undress baby and begin cleaning the least dirty areas first: hair/head, face, neck, hands. Take wet washcloth,

apply a small amount of baby soap to washcloth, and gently wash neck, hands, and face. Then rinse and wring out washcloth. Wipe soap off baby.

5. Next clean arms, legs, trunk of body, and folds of baby's skin.

6. When you're ready to clean baby's bottom, remove diaper (air acts as a stimulant to urination, especially in boys). Use the second washcloth to clean baby's bottom (definitely the dirtiest area!).

7. To ensure baby stays warm and comfortable, place the hooded towel over the body parts not being washed.

8. When you're through wiping down, gently wrap your baby in the hooded towel and pat dry.

9. Be careful of the umbilical cord (do not get it wet until the stump falls off) and clean it well with alcohol pads or sterile cotton.

10. If your son has been circumcised, then carefully dry the penis and apply topical antibiotic ointment and gauze pad.

11. Very carefully clean the *outer* ears with cotton tip applicator. Never probe into the ear canal.

12. Diaper and dress baby.

13. A good cuddle is now in order!

14. Don't go outdoors with baby immediately after sponge bath as you may risk giving the baby a chill.

Bathtub

Some people prefer bathing baby in the bathroom, while others prefer a large kitchen sink. You must decide what is most comfortable for you and baby. If you choose the kitchen sink, you'll need a big bath sponge. If you bathe baby in the bathroom, use a plastic baby tub with large bath sponge that fits inside baby tub. Bath water should be warm but not hot. Always test the water before immersing the child. Remember to keep the water level shallow.

Babies are quite active in the tub. You may want to wear a plastic-covered apron to keep yourself dry. Have all your bathing supplies at your fingertips. These include:

- Plastic baby tub with large bath sponge that fits into baby tub

- Baby soap and shampoo

- Two washcloths

- Hooded towel

- Baby powder

- Baby moisturizing cream (hypoallergenic)

- Cotton tip applicators

- Diaper

- Diaper rash ointment

- Baby toy

- Change of clothing

- Baby brush and comb

- Baby scissors and soft emery board

Here are some suggestions to follow when bathing baby:

1. Do not bathe baby immediately after feedings; this can upset his full tummy and cause him to spit up.

2. If possible, give baths in the late afternoon. The bath is soothing and relaxing and becomes a good preparation for a peaceful sleep.

3. Turn on the answering machine or don't answer the phone. There should be no distractions during bath time.

4. The bathroom should be warm. A cool room can lead to chills.

5. Test the water with your elbow before placing baby in the tub.

6. Remember to support baby's head while you gently wash him with a washcloth and baby soap. Wash the face with a wet washcloth—no soap, please!

7. Clean the least dirty areas first: neck, hands, and face.

8. Carefully wash and massage baby's scalp daily. You may notice a soft spot at the top of his head (anterior fontanelle), so massage gently. This spot will close by the time he is eighteen months old. If dryness occurs, consult your pediatrician because your child could have *cradle cap.*

9. Wash baby girl's genital area with warm water only, front to back. If baby boy has not been circumcised, do not retract the foreskin. Consult your pediatrician as to when the foreskin is fully separated and can be retracted without injury. Carefully wash the penis with soap and water.

10. To distract baby, have a water toy or rattle available.

11. Clean behind the ears with the wet washcloth and use a damp cotton tip applicator to clean *outer* ear. Never probe into the ear canal.

PINK AND BLUE HINT

To avoid getting shampoo and water in your baby's or toddler's eyes, use a bath bonnet that fits comfortably on the child's forehead.

PINK AND BLUE HINT

Bath time is a good time to give baby a daily dose of vitamins.

PINK AND BLUE HINT

You can cut baby's nails now, or if you prefer, do so when baby is asleep and more relaxed. (Baby's nails don't harden until about three weeks after birth. While nails are soft, hook baby's finger over your finger and gently file with soft side of an emery board. Once the nails harden, you can use baby scissors.)

12. After the bath, wrap baby in a towel and dry well. Then massage cream all over the body, and if there's a diaper rash, apply ointment. Follow this with baby powder.

13. Diaper and dress baby.

14. Cuddle your baby to impart a warm, secure feeling.

15. Stay indoors for a while after the bath. If you take baby outside immediately, a chill may result.

Diapering

Like it or not, you've got to do it! Now that you have a baby, diapering is obviously one of your most important daily tasks. If you don't know how to diaper, you can practice on a doll or ask a friend who has a baby to show you the technique. The hospital nursing staff will also teach you how to diaper.

Remember to change your baby whenever a diaper is wet or dirty. This is good personal hygiene and helps baby avoid nasty diaper rashes. If you have a boy, keep the penis covered while diapering, because air is a stimulant for urinating. When diapering a girl, be sure to wipe the vaginal area from front to back. Keep a rattle or stuffed animal on your changing table to occupy your baby while you're diapering.

Diaper Choices

There are two kinds of diapers: cloth and disposable. The type of diaper you select is an individual choice. There are advantages and disadvantages to each.

Advantages of Cloth Diapers

☼ They are environmentally safe.

☀ They are less expensive.

☀ They are gentler on newborn's skin.

☀ If you use a diaper service, you won't need to purchase and care for diapers. The service conveniently picks up and delivers supplies weekly.

☀ If you use a diaper service, the diapers will be laundered with nonchemical protective agents that slow down bacterial growth.

Disadvantages of Cloth Diapers

☀ Cloth diapers are less absorbent, and you need to change baby more frequently.

☀ If you don't use a diaper service, you must purchase a large quantity of diapers; maintenance and care are very time consuming.

☀ Odor from dirty diapers is unavoidable, even with strong deodorizers. (However, if you use a diaper service, usually their deodorizers are more powerful.)

☀ Cloth diapers are leakier and messier. There is a higher chance of fecal contamination.

☀ You will need to purchase Velcro covers and/or diaper pins and plastic covers. This is an additional expense.

☀ Diaper pins can stick you and baby.

☀ It takes more time preparing and changing baby.

☀ As your child becomes more active, the cloth diaper process is more cumbersome.

☀ Day care centers don't always allow cloth diapers.

Advantages of Disposable Diapers

❦ They are more convenient and make changing baby faster and easier.

❦ They are more absorbent.

❦ You don't need to purchase the cloth diaper accessories, such as Velcro covers, diaper pins, and cloth covers.

❦ As baby reaches toddler stage, disposable diapers are quicker to put on and remove.

❦ Foul odor will not linger since disposable diapers are thrown out.

❦ Most day care centers allow only disposable diapers.

❦ Reduced chance of fecal contamination.

Disadvantages of Disposable Diapers

❦ Disposable diapers are not biodegradable and, therefore, are not friendly to the environment.

❦ They are more costly, and therefore, there is a tendency to change less frequently.

❦ They are not as gentle on a newborn's skin as cotton diapers.

❦ It is difficult to detect wetness until the diaper is saturated. If baby is not changed quickly, rashes will result.

Steps to Follow for Diapering

❦ Have all your supplies close at hand. These items should include:

⊚ Clean diapers (with diaper liners and Velcro diaper covers or pins, if using cloth)

⊚ Medicated baby powder or cornstarch in a shaker

⊚ Diaper rash emollient

⊚ Petroleum jelly

⊚ Sterilized cotton

⊚ Warm, wet washcloth (can be used in place of diaper wipes)

⊚ Diaper wipes (use after baby reaches one month old, but discontinue use if rash or redness occurs)

⊚ Tissues

⊚ Hypoallergenic moisturizing cream

⊚ Alcohol pads or alcohol (for umbilicus care)

⊚ Gauze pads and topical antibiotic ointment (for circumcised penis)

☼ Throw wet disposable diaper into deodorized diaper pail. For cloth diapers, throw liner into pail and cloth diaper into a separate diaper hamper.

☼ If baby has a bowel movement, put the dirty diaper or liner aside for the moment and continue to diaper. When you're done, place baby in the crib and dispose of the stool in the toilet. Throw disposable diaper into the diaper pail. If using cloth diapers, the stool and liner can be flushed together. Cloth diaper should go into diaper hamper. This procedure will help prevent a terrible odor in baby's room.

☀ Clean baby's bottom very well with either diaper wipes, moisturizing cream with cotton balls, or washcloth. Blot dry with tissues.

☀ Slip clean diaper under baby's bottom. If rash is present, apply a thick coat of diaper rash emollient. If baby's bottom is fine, use a small amount of petroleum jelly, then sprinkle with powder or cornstarch.

☀ To prepare a cloth diaper, fold diaper into triangular shape. Add liner, place on top of opened diaper cover, and fasten Velcro tabs at baby's waist, or fasten all three diaper corners with a strong diaper pin, and put on plastic diaper cover.

☀ Diaper covers can be obtained through your diaper service, baby specialty shop, baby care mail-order catalogues, and some department stores.

☀ To prepare a disposable diaper, lay baby on top half of diaper. Fold bottom half up and over pelvic area; fasten with tape from back to front.

Dressing: Six Months and Older

How you dress your baby should be appropriate for both the occasion and climate. Always bring along an extra set of clothes and a sweatshirt or sweater. It's best to be prepared! Remember, when your child is in a stroller, he is inactive and will feel colder than you do. That's why it's a good idea to have an extra blanket and jacket available. All of this can be placed in your well-packed diaper bag.

To build your child's wardrobe, check with friends and family for hand-me-down clothing. If the garments are clean, they are fine. There are also second-hand clothing shops in most towns and cities. A unisex wardrobe should include some of the following:

- ❦ Overalls (preferably with snap crotch)

- ❦ Elastic waistband pants or shorts (sweatpants material is great)

- ❦ Washable tee shirts

- ❦ Sweatshirts

- ❦ One-piece jumpsuits, without feet (preferably with snap crotch or zipper front)

- ❦ Six undershirts

- ❦ Six pairs of socks

- ❦ Three to six pairs of training underpants (to be worn in place of diapers when toilet training begins)

- ❦ Three to six pairs of pajamas (If your child is a restless sleeper, the blanket sleeper pajama or the blanket sleeping bag is a good solution.)

- ❦ Jacket (appropriate for your local climate)

- ❦ Hooded raincoat and rain boots (no umbrellas at this age)

- ❦ Two hats (one summer-weight and one winter-weight)

- ❦ A snowsuit and accessories (for cold weather climate)

- ❦ Party clothes for special occasions

- ❦ Shoes (These are only to be worn when your child walks with confidence. When you're ready to purchase your child's first pair of shoes, consult your pediatrician for recommendations.)

PINK AND BLUE HINT

Save baby's first pair of shoes and have them bronzed at your local children's shoe store. They make wonderful bookends!

Washing Baby's Clothing

For the first six months, keep baby's laundry separate from the rest of the family's. It's best to wash baby's laundry in mild hypoallergenic washing detergent because it isn't harsh on baby's skin. Select a mild bleach for really soiled items. As baby gets older, use a low-suds, no-enzyme detergent that's good for the whole family.

Time-Tested Advice

* For formula, stool, and other stubborn stains, soak the items first in a mixture of one gallon of cold water and one-quarter cup nonchlorine bleach for about fifteen to twenty minutes. Be sure to mix the bleach and water well before adding garments. Then rinse with water and wash as usual with other laundry. Wear rubber gloves when working with bleach.

* For a medium to large load of stained and extra-dirty items, use one cup of detergent and a half-cup of bleach. First add soap and make sure it is completely agitated. Then add bleach to the soapy water and let all ingredients mix thoroughly for one to two minutes. Now add laundry. This formula can be cut proportionally for a smaller load. Fabric softener is optional.

* For an all white wash, follow the same formula but use hot water.

❧ Don't bleach red garments because they usually run. (You can bleach black, but it tends to fade with numerous washings.)

❧ If you're hesitant about using bleach because of baby's sensitive skin, rewash the bleached items in a new soapy cycle.

꩜ 10 ꩜

Sleep

One of the major priorities in baby's life is establishing good routines. Once you've come home from the hospital, you need to get your baby on a sleeping and eating schedule. Establishing a routine may seem difficult at first, but it is extremely important for your baby's healthy development—and your sanity. A structured environment provides baby with a sense of security that will be of benefit throughout life. Sleep itself is a physiological necessity. Regardless of temperament, your child can be taught good sleeping habits with consistent behavior and constant reinforcement on your part.

For the first four to six weeks of life, it's a good idea to have your baby sleep in a bassinet or portable crib in your bedroom. It's convenient for middle-of-the-night feedings and gives baby and parents a sense of security and togetherness. During the day, the bassinet can be moved to baby's room

PINK AND BLUE ALERT

Due to recent data, parents are advised to put their babies (up to eight months of age) to sleep on either their side or back.

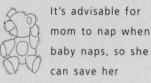

(see Chapter 4, "Creating Baby's Room") or any room in the house.

While some parents would prefer baby to sleep in bed with them, it's not a good idea. From the beginning, you must establish a precedent of sleeping apart from baby. In the first few months, however, it is perfectly acceptable to feed baby for middle-of-the-night feedings in your bed as a matter of convenience. Once you have burped and comforted baby, return the little one to the bassinet or crib.

Birth to Eight Weeks

The first two months are often an erratic and frustrating time for a newborn's family because of the experimenting with baby's eating and sleeping schedules. Your main goal is to teach baby the difference between day and night. Keeping baby's room naturally lit for daytime naps will help her recognize that it is daytime. Don't close curtains, shutters, or blinds. If she sleeps more than three to four hours during the day, wake her up, but don't deny her daytime naps. If she becomes overtired, she may not sleep as well at night. Play with baby while she's awake, but don't overstimulate her.

Daytime household activities such as vacuuming, operating washers, dryers, and dishwashers and noises such as barking dogs, ringing phones, and chiming doorbells should not stop because baby is napping. Don't tiptoe around the house or speak in whispers. Baby needs to adapt to your environment and noise level, not you to hers.

Pacifiers

All babies have an innate urge to suck. Once you know your baby has had enough to eat but still needs to suck, try giving her a pacifier. There are many types and sizes to choose from. Let your baby be the connoisseur! There are some differences of opinion about how often to use pacifiers and how long they should be used, so speak to your pediatrician and listen to suggestions. If you decide to use pacifiers, here are some guidelines:

🌟 Don't use a pacifier that is too large and obstructs baby's nasal passage.

🌟 Use only one-piece models that cannot separate, break, and choke baby.

🌟 Make sure the pacifier base has ventilation holes.

🌟 Do not make a pacifier necklace or put a long string through the pacifier because baby can be choked or strangled.

🌟 Don't put sweeteners of any kind on pacifier to encourage its use.

🌟 Make sure you keep enough pacifiers on hand in case they get lost or chewed up.

🌟 Try to limit the use only to sleep time.

Time-Tested Advice

Here are some suggestions to enhance baby's sleep time:

💜 Follow the same routine every night at bedtime— turn off or dim lights, sing a song, or play soft music.

💜 Bedtime should be a calm, winding-down period. Baby will learn to associate nighttime with bedtime.

- Keep lights dimmed for middle-of-the-night feedings and diaper changes.

- Don't encourage too much contact and stimulation in the middle of the night because this can affect sleep patterns.

- Never wake your baby up in the middle of the night! If she does awaken, give her the breast or bottle (keeping lights dim) and put her back to bed.

- Play recorded tapes that recreate the sound of a mother's womb and heartbeat (available at baby specialty shops and some record stores).

- Give baby a warm bath and nice massage to calm her down before nap time or bedtime.

- Cuddle baby and rock her to sleep.

- Keep room temperature at a comfortable setting— not too hot and not too cold.

- Make sure sleepwear and diaper do not fit too tightly.

- If infant has difficulty going back to sleep after a middle-of-the-night feeding, allow her to rest on your chest or abdomen. You can also wrap her securely in a blanket; this is a reassuring feeling. As she's drifting off to sleep, put her back in the crib.

PINK AND BLUE HINT

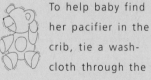

To help baby find her pacifier in the crib, tie a washcloth through the handle. Baby can easily grasp and find it.

Eight to Twelve Weeks

Many babies begin to sleep through the night when they're about eight to twelve weeks old or eleven to twelve pounds. If your baby has attained this age or weight but is still waking up for a middle-of-the-night feeding, don't give up hope. It's perfectly OK. Just continue following the suggestions for Birth to Eight Weeks until baby progresses to the next stage.

Twelve to Sixteen Weeks

Once your baby reaches sixteen weeks (four months) she should be able to sleep through the night. To ease your baby into this next phase, try feeding her around 7:00 P.M. and then again at approximately 11:00 P.M. Baby should then be able to go at least seven to eight hours with uninterrupted sleep. At this age and stage, it will become easier to plan a daily schedule.

It's not unusual for an infant to fuss or cry in the middle of the night, since she has grown accustomed to that feeding. But her fussing is more out of habit than need. If you give in to baby's crying and reward her with the breast or bottle, she'll continue doing this every night. Instead, rub her back, use a pacifier (with your doctor's approval), sing a song, or talk softly to her. As with a younger baby, don't stimulate her by picking her up or walking her around. This will only create more bad habits that you'll eventually have to break. Baby's wakefulness and fretfulness will decrease in time if you're patient. Feel confident in the steps you're taking—baby can detect a parent's uncertainties and apprehensions.

If, after one week, you're unsuccessful in getting baby to sleep through the night, consult your pediatrician.

PINK AND BLUE HINT

A good strategy to get baby to sleep through the night is to begin by appeasing her with a pacifier, talking to her softly, or rubbing her back for no longer than ten minutes. Repeat this procedure, reducing a minute every night. The result should be a baby who sleeps through the night.

Naps

When your baby is three to four months old, nap time will be more clearly defined. Until now, your infant has spent the majority of each day sleeping. As baby gets older, she will probably take two naps, one in the morning and one in the afternoon. One nap is usually longer than the other. Some babies, however, will take multiple catnaps lasting no more than twenty to forty-five minutes. Whatever the case, your baby should nap regularly. A baby who stays awake all day becomes overtired and cranky in the late afternoon or dinnertime, which throws off her whole bedtime schedule. If your baby never naps during the day, it's likely she'll be so overtired that even falling asleep at night becomes impossible. If your baby refuses napping altogether, try a ride in the car, a walk in the stroller, or a warm bath. Sometimes just taking the baby outside in the fresh air can help induce sleep.

Four to Six Months

The following is a sample schedule of what baby's daily routine might be (keep in mind that breast-fed babies may need to eat more often):

7:00 to 7:30 A.M.: Baby awakens and is breast-fed or bottle-fed. Baby will probably stay awake for about two hours. This is a good time for her to play in the playpen.

10:30 to 11:00 A.M.: Baby gets fed again and then can nap.

12:00 to 12:30 P.M.: A good time to go out with baby and run some errands. Or, just use it as more playtime.

1:30 to 2:00 P.M.: Baby gets fed again.

2:00 to 2:30 P.M.: Baby takes another nap (usually longer than morning nap).

4:30 P.M. (or when baby awakens): Bottle-fed baby can get four ounces of diluted juice. Breast-fed baby gets another feeding. Late afternoon baths are great to calm baby down for nighttime sleep (if you haven't given her a bath in the morning).

7:00 to 7:30 P.M.: Baby gets fed for the last time today.

8:00 to 8:30 P.M.: Time for bed.

Six to Nine Months

Again, this is only a sample schedule. Your child may awaken earlier or later. Adjust your time intervals accordingly.

7:00 to 7:30 A.M.: Baby awakens and is breast-fed or bottle-fed.

8:00 to 8:15 A.M.: A six-month-old now starts solid foods (see Chapter 11, "Solid Food"). Allow thirty to forty-five minutes between breast or bottle and breakfast so baby can digest.

10:00 to 10:30 A.M.: Baby takes a morning nap.

12:00 P.M.: Baby awakens and gets breast or bottle, followed thirty to forty-five minutes later with lunch. (After eating is a good time to take baby out or play with her.)

2:00 to 2:30 P.M.: Baby takes afternoon nap.

4:00 P.M. (or when baby awakens): Baby gets a bottle of diluted juice.

5:00 P.M.: Baby takes a bath.

5:30 to 6:00 P.M.: Baby eats dinner and has part of bottle or breast-feeding.

7:00 to 7:30 P.M.: Baby finishes breast or bottle and goes to sleep for the night.

At this point in a baby's life, you will have to learn to be flexible about her schedule. Each child has different sleeping needs.

Nine Months and Older

At nine months of age, your baby may no longer require two naps a day. Once again, you will be readjusting her daily schedule. If she needs only one daily nap, it may fall around midday. Suggestions for scheduling are:

❂ Lunch at 11:30 A.M. or noon and nap afterward

❂ Nap at 11:00-11:30 A.M. (depending on morning wake-up time) and a late lunch

When baby wakes up early in the morning, don't immediately rush into her room. Allow her time to be alone in the crib and entertain herself. You'll be delighted with the joyful sounds she makes!

Time-Tested Advice

If your baby or toddler is experiencing sleep difficulties either at bedtime or nap time, try some of the following ideas:

- Don't let your child sleep more than three hours in the afternoon if it affects her nighttime sleep patterns.

- Your toddler may resist taking any naps, but remember she can become overtired and have difficulty sleeping at night. Don't give in so easily; encourage her to take a nap. Try putting her favorite stuffed animal into bed with her, and make believe it's nap time for both of them.

- Avoid very active play or overstimulation just before bedtime.

- To calm baby, try giving her a warm bath, followed by a gentle massage.

- Sit together in a quiet place and look at books.

- Cuddle baby and rock her to sleep.

- Make sure your child's room is kept at a comfortable temperature.

- Make sure sleepwear and diaper are not too tight.

- If baby is a restless sleeper and the covers come undone, try a blanket sleeping bag or blanket sleeper pajamas (available in all sizes).

- If the sun seems to be the cause for early wake-ups, try blackout blinds or curtains.

❧ 11 ❧

Solid Food

For the first six months of baby's life, preparing food has not been an especially creative cooking experience. Now's your chance to get out your apron and blend, puree, grind, or whip up some simple culinary delights for your baby's extremely discriminating taste buds. This is a fun phase for the two of you. Keep your camera loaded and ready to catch the moment! If your baby doesn't like the taste or texture of something the first time you feed it to him, don't give up. With a few repeated tries, he may grow to love it. Your baby's diet is very important. Good nutrition is essential to his growth and development. It also forms the foundation for his eating habits later in life.

Cooking and Feeding Solid Food: Six to Ten Months

While you won't be serving complicated cuisine, you will be introducing a wide variety of cereals, fruits, vegetables, and eventually meat, chicken, and fish. If you don't already own a blender, grinder, or food processor, this is a good time to invest in one. Begin feeding baby foods with smooth consistencies. Gradually prepare the food a little bit thicker and grainier as baby's palate accepts it; this should be around the seventh month or when baby gets more teeth.

Whether your child is breast-fed or bottle-fed, he's been receiving sufficient calorie intake. Now that he's getting bigger, your baby needs more calories, fat, carbohydrates, and natural vitamin C from other sources.

Foods should be introduced one at a time at either breakfast or lunch, and each new food should be repeated for three consecutive days before moving on to the next one. This way, you can easily recognize whether your baby is allergic to a particular food. Food allergies can manifest themselves as diarrhea, rashes, or vomiting. If your baby has any reaction to a new food, call your pediatrician immediately.

Time-Tested Advice

* When preparing baby food, don't add seasonings such as sugar, honey, salt, or pepper.

* Make a large enough quantity so that it can be poured into an 18-slot plastic ice cube tray (each cube holds one tablespoon) and frozen.

❧ Allow food to cool before putting it in the ice tray. Then cover with plastic wrap and place in the freezer. Each tray should hold only one type of food.

❧ Once frozen, put cubes of the same food in an airtight plastic freezer bag. Mark the type of food and the date on the bag.

❧ Make one shelf in your freezer strictly for baby's food, always keeping packages with the oldest dates to the front. Food frozen in this manner is good for up to two months.

❧ All foods can be served warm, except for cereals and fruits, which should be served at room temperature.

❧ A baby's heating dish is great—just be sure to remove the electric plug before serving!

❧ Frozen food should not be left out to defrost for long periods of time because bacteria can form. Defrost food in the refrigerator three hours prior to serving or use the warming dish to defrost quickly.

❧ Feed baby with a baby spoon that has a long handle and rubber-coated mouth; it makes feeding time much easier.

❧ Never put solid food in a bottle!

❧ Always test the temperature of the food before feeding baby!

❧ Keep food out of baby's reach—it will be tempting to play with.

❧ Never feed baby in a hurry!

PINK AND BLUE ALERT

 Do not use honey in baby's food because it can cause botulism in infants and toddlers.

PINK AND BLUE ALERT

 Don't leave baby alone or unattended while he's eating because he can choke on the food.

PINK AND BLUE ALERT

 Baby's skin can turn a yellowish tone if he eats too much of a yellow vegetable. If this happens, consult your doctor immediately.

PINK AND BLUE ALERT

 Fruits are fine to eat twice a day, but vegetables should be served only once.

PINK AND BLUE ALERT

Remember, don't give baby a bottle in the crib!

Basic Schedule

Solid foods should be given to your six-month-old twice daily at breakfast and dinner. Here's a sample first feeding schedule:

6:30 to 7:00 A.M.: Breast or 8-ounce bottle of formula

7:45 to 8:00 A.M.: Breakfast (cereal)

11:30 to noon: Breast or 8-ounce bottle of formula

3:00 to 4:00 P.M.: 4-ounce bottle of diluted juice (apple, cranberry, grape, or pear)

5:30 to 6:00 P.M.: Dinner (cereal)

7:00 P.M. or bedtime: Breast or 8-ounce bottle of formula

Introduction and Preparation of Solid Food

Feed your child until he is full and satisfied. He'll be the best judge of how much he wants to eat. The following chart is a guideline for the introduction and preparation of food, starting with a six-month-old child:

AGE	FOOD	PREPARATION
6 months	rice cereal	Mix cereal with a little formula or breast milk (not too thick or too thin).
6 months	⅓ banana (ripe)	Mash with fork or use baby food grinder.
6 months	applesauce	Put peeled, seeded apples with small amount of water in blender and puree, or cook apples with water to desired softness and puree.
6 months	pear	Blend or puree peeled, seeded, ripe pears with small amount of water, or cook pears with water to desired softness and puree.
6 months	rice cereal with banana, applesauce, or pear	Upon accepting rice cereal, introduce new cereals one at a time. Choices are barley, oatmeal, or mixed cereal. For a variety, mix a cereal with one or more fruits.
6 months	peach, apricot	Cook peeled, seeded fruit with small amount of water, or steam fruit to desired softness and puree.
6 months	papaya	Don't cook this fruit. For best results, use a blender or grinder with a tiny amount of water. Don't mash with fork because papaya is too stringy.

AGE	FOOD	PREPARATION
6 months	orange/yellow vegetables: acorn squash,banana squash, carrots	Steam or boil vegetables; then puree.
6 months	orange/yellow vegetables: carrots, acorn and crookneck squash, yams, potatoes (red, white, sweet)	Steam or boil vegetables, then puree. Potatoes can be baked, then pureed.
6 months	green, leafy vegetables: green beans (remove strings), peas, spinach, zucchini, summer squash	Steam vegetables; then puree.
7 months	meat: ground beef (lean)	Ask the butcher to grind the meat extra-fine. If there's gristle, remove it. Sauté meat until pink, then add small amount of water. Simmer 5 minutes covered. Put meat and liquid into grinder or food processor. The consistency will be smooth enough for baby's palate.
7 months	ground lamb	Use same method as for ground beef. Or broil lamp chop (discard fat), then add water and grind to a smooth texture. The eye of the chop is the most tender portion.

AGE	FOOD	PREPARATION
7 months	ground veal	Use same method as for ground beef, or broil veal chop and follow lamb chop recipe. Or bake boneless veal cutlets and grind with small amount of water, as you do with other meats.
7 months	chicken or turkey (pieces or ground)	Poach chicken with carrots, celery, and potatoes. Remove chicken bones and skin, and grind chicken with small amount of poaching liquid. Blend or puree vegetables (except celery, which is too stringy and should be removed), and your whole meal for baby is complete. Chicken can also be baked forty-five minutes to one hour and then ground with a small amount of water. This method is great when the family is eating baked chicken, too. The same method can be applied to turkey parts, but you'll need more cooking time depending on the size of the part. If using ground chicken or turkey, follow the recipe for ground meats.
7 months	fish (do not use shellfish)	Types of fish suggested are: sole, red snapper, flounder, halibut, bass, white fish, and salmon. All fish must be filleted *very* carefully. Poach or bake fish, and puree with

AGE	FOOD	PREPARATION
		small amount of water. Don't use poaching liquid because the taste may be too strong.
7 months	plain yogurt	Mix your pureed fruit with yogurt. Try using less fruit to start.
7 months	low-fat cottage cheese	Mash with fork or put through grinder or blender.
7 months	egg yolk	Hard-boil egg. Remove egg yolk and mash into cereal. Serve three times a week.

Daily Diet Planning: Eight to Ten Months

At eight months, continue with the foods you've already introduced and increase the quantity. Your child can now have two fruits and two vegetables per day, and he should be eating three complete meals. This is a good time for him to start using a spoon. The following is a sample menu planner.

	BREAKFAST	LUNCH	DINNER
Sun.	rice cereal with banana	1 cube ground beef, 1 cube banana squash, 1 cube green beans	cottage cheese and peaches
Mon.	oatmeal with apple-sauce and egg yolk	1 cube chicken, 1 cube carrots, 1 cube peas	yogurt and bananas
Tue.	barley with pears	1 cube lamb, 1 cube sweet potato, 1 cube spinach	rice cereal with apricots
Wed.	mixed cereal with papaya	1 cube fish, 1 cube acorn squash, 1 cube zucchini	cottage cheese and pears
Thur.	rice cereal with applesauce and egg yolk	1 cube turkey, 1 cube (red or white) potato, 1 cube crookneck squash	yogurt and peaches
Fri.	oatmeal with apricots	1 cube veal, 1 cube carrots, 1 cube green peas	barley cereal with applesauce
Sat.	mixed cereal with peaches and pears	1 cube chicken, 1 cube spinach, 1 cube yams	yogurt and papaya

At ten months, follow the eight-month menu, increasing the quantity of food. Baby can start to eat a whole egg prepared scrambled, poached, soft-boiled (three minutes), or hard-boiled. It is now time to advance to "junior foods"— lumpier food. This means the consistency becomes thicker. Instead of using the blender or the grinder, mash the food with a fork. Introduce mashed foods one at a time so that baby's palate gets accustomed to the new texture.

Finger Foods: Ten Months to One Year

At ten months, baby can begin to feed himself finger foods. Don't overload his plate with too much food; start with small portions of one or two items. Take into consideration the number of teeth baby has. Make pieces large enough for him to pick up by himself, but small enough for him to chew easily and digest. Don't add spices until baby has accepted the new foods. Feeding himself will be a whole new pleasurable experience!

There are many good bite-sized finger foods. Here are some suggestions:

Breads: plain or whole-wheat bagel, thinly sliced whole-wheat (if baby has no wheat allergies), sourdough, egg, seedless rye. Always remove crust from bread.

Cereals: O-shaped, rice puffs, corn puffs (with no added sugar or salt)

Cheese: mild cheddar, domestic Swiss, Monterey Jack, muenster, mozzarella, gouda, cottage cheese (avoid processed cheeses)

Cooked vegetables: carrots, zucchini, beets, potatoes (white, red, sweet, or yam), spinach, broccoli, cauliflower, peas (cut in half)

Eggs: scrambled, sunny-side-up, hard-boiled (cut into bite-sized pieces)

Fish: anything flaky and well-filleted (no shellfish, and beware of fish from contaminated waters)

Fruits: ripe banana, very ripe pear, cooked apple, peach, cantaloupe, apricot, mango, seedless watermelon, papaya, nectarine, kiwi, avocado (for now, remove skin from all fruits)

Meat and poultry: cut across the grain into small, bite-sized pieces

Pastas: cooked penne, rigatoni, rotelle, ziti (cut in small pieces for easy chewing and grasping)

PINK AND BLUE ALERT

If gagging occurs, put your finger into the baby's mouth and remove all residual food.

If your baby is still hungry after his meal, talk to your pediatrician about increasing the quantity. As baby is more accepting of foods, you can become more creative. Here are some additional food ideas:

Finger sandwiches: Use cookie cutters and make different shaped sandwiches to hold baby's attention (remove crust).

Finger sandwich fillers: tuna (mashed very fine), melted cheese, jelly and creamy-style peanut butter or any nut butter (spread lightly because it's sticky on the palate), egg salad, apple butter, mashed avocado

French toast: Cut in small pieces.

Pancakes or waffles: plain or whole-wheat, banana, berry, apple (if no known allergies exist for wheat and berries)

Pastas: Cook with light, non-spicy tomato sauce or cheese.

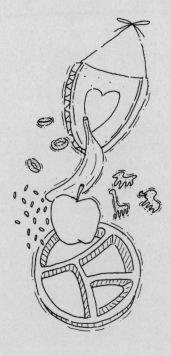

Food for Fifteen Months and Older

A fifteen-month-old child can eat just about anything. Give him the same meal you prepare for the rest of the family. Remember to cut everything into small pieces. This is also a good time to introduce your child to different ethnic foods and spices that your family already enjoys. Avoid fried foods and butter because you want to keep baby's cholesterol at a healthy level. Also, don't add sugar or salt to foods to encourage baby to eat. If he eats sufficient amounts of fresh fruits and vegetables, he will get the natural sugars his body requires. Excessive salt can lead to high blood pressure in adult life.

Additional breakfast ideas are:

- **Fruit smoothie:** four ounces orange juice, two tablespoons yogurt, half a banana mixed in blender (substitute any fruits and juices your baby likes)

- **Pancakes:** plain or whole-wheat with fruit (blueberry, apple, or banana)

- **Cereals:** O-shaped cereals, iron-fortified cereal, rice or corn puffs, cooked creamy wheat or oatmeal

- Toast with cottage cheese and sprinkled cinnamon

- Bowl of sliced mixed fruit

- Pita bread with melted cheese

- Seedless rye, wheat, or sourdough toast thinly spread with creamy-style peanut butter (or any nut butter) and jelly

- Toasted English muffin spread with apple butter

- Any fruit or vegetable muffin (no nuts), banana, date, or applesauce breads (no nuts), biscuits (not too thick)

Additional lunch and dinner ideas:

- Grilled cheese with tomato (and avocado)

- **Quesadillas:** melted cheese on flour tortilla

- Tuna melt

- **Egg salad:** prepared with small amount of plain yogurt (no celery)

- Peanut butter or any nut butter (creamy style) and jelly

- Thinly sliced turkey or chicken in pita bread or on any favorite bread

- Skinless turkey or chicken dogs: 100% meat with no fillers or sodium

- **Omelets:** using any cheese or vegetable

- **Pizza:** make your own with English muffins, tomato sauce, and mozzarella cheese

- Fruit salad, cottage cheese, or yogurt

- Egg noodles, cottage cheese, and cinnamon baked in oven

- Chicken or turkey salad (no celery)

- Any pasta dish with your favorite sauce

- Baked potato with plain yogurt (no butter)

- **Soups:** start with warm, clear broths, slowly adding cooked noodles and cooked vegetables

- Soup and sandwich

- Banana bread, date bread, orange bread, zucchini bread, applesauce bread (no nuts) lightly spread with cream cheese

PINK AND BLUE HINT

For clear soups, try serving with a straw. A spoon may be too difficult to use with soup.

These menu planners should be used as a guideline. You may want to switch the lunch and dinner suggestions depending on your family's schedule.

	BREAKFAST	LUNCH	DINNER
Sun.	waffles or French toast, sliced fruit	peanut butter, sliced bananas on whole wheat	turkey, yams, zucchini
Mon.	scrambled eggs, toast, or bagel	hamburger, piece of cheese, fruit	pasta with tomato sauce, broccoli
Tue.	O-shaped cereal, fruit smoothie	grilled cheese, cooked carrots, frozen yogurt	fish, rice, beets
Wed.	warm cereal, fruit, cinnamon toast	tuna sandwich, sliced avocado	lamb chop, baked potato, peas
Thur.	soft or poached egg, toast or bagel, and fruit	chicken soup with pieces of chicken and vegetables	pasta with meat sauce, spinach
Fri.	banana pancakes, yogurt	fish, mashed potatoes, acorn squash	pizza, zucchini
Sat.	cereal with fruit	noodles and cottage cheese baked in oven, applesauce	chicken, carrots, red potatoes

Food Safety

Never leave your child unattended while he's eating. This is the most important rule in food safety. Little eaters can choke easily. Any adult feeding your child should be trained in CPR (cardiopulmonary resuscitation). If baby starts to choke, remember to stay calm—don't panic!

Consult your pediatrician for additional food safety recommendations and procedures. The following should be standard household rules:

1. Always sit down while eating or drinking.

2. Chew food well and slowly.

3. No talking while chewing food.

4. Don't walk or run with food on a stick, such as lollipops and Popsicles.

5. No eating in a moving car.

The following foods are not safe for a child under two-and-a-half years old:

❦ Raw carrots, celery, whole peas, corn

❦ Raw apples, pears, grapes

❦ Chips, pretzels, popcorn, peanuts (or any nuts)

❦ Meat chunks

❦ Bread sticks

❦ Bagels with seeds

❦ Hard candy

❦ Raisins

There are certain foods children can be allergic to, especially if there's a family history of allergies. Discuss this with

PINK AND BLUE ALERT
If food cannot be dislodged from baby's mouth with your fingers, then put him over your forearm with head down and deliver a few soft but firm blows between his shoulder blades. Don't administer the Heimlich maneuver to babies under one year of age.

PINK AND BLUE HINT
Read all labels and check ingredients before serving your child prepared foods. Make sure they are free of ingredients your child is allergic to.

your pediatrician. Also inform him of any family history of coronary artery disease, so he will monitor your child's cholesterol level as he grows older.

The foods that commonly cause allergic reactions are:

- ❦ Milk, eggs, egg whites, dairy products

- ❦ Wheat products

- ❦ Berries and citrus fruits

- ❦ Tomatoes, corn

- ❦ Chocolate

- ❦ Shellfish (shrimp, crab, clams, oysters, scallops, lobster)

- ❦ Pork products (bacon, ham, sausage)

- ❦ Cinnamon

Food Snacks

Food snacks should be offered mid-morning and mid-afternoon. If your child has breakfast at 7:30 to 8:00 A.M. and lunch at noon, then a light snack at 10:00 A.M. is fine. An afternoon snack can be given to your child after he wakes up from his nap. Serve the snack with juice or milk. This is a good time for baby to practice using a training cup.

Some snack ideas for children aged eighteen months and older are:

- ❦ Creamy peanut butter and bananas (very ripe), skinless apples

- ❦ Cheese and seedless crackers

- ❦ Any sliced fruit

- ❦ Vegetables cut up with a simple yogurt or avocado dip (dipping is fun for children)

- ❦ Unsalted rice cakes with apple butter or creamy nut butter

- ❦ O-shaped cereal and sliced fruit

- ❦ Applesauce

- ❦ Frozen yogurt (feels great on sore, teething gums)

- ❦ Homemade natural frozen fruit juice pops (dilute the juice)

- ❦ Rice pudding

- ❦ Baked apple (no skin)

- ❦ Bananas dipped in yogurt

- ❦ Healthy cookies, such as plain graham crackers (serve sugary cookies only as a special treat)

Restaurant Dining

The key to eating out with your baby or toddler is to be prepared. It's probably easier taking baby out when he's sleeping if you can count on his usual sleep schedule, and he's not bothered by excessive moving or noise. Choose a restaurant that not only is accommodating to families, but also provides quick and efficient service. Don't be offended if you're seated in the back of the restaurant; you'll be farther away from other people and less likely to disturb their meal. For now, don't plan on long, romantic dinners with baby. When he's off to college you'll have plenty of time alone!

For your convenience, you should have a well-prepared baby bag whenever you go out. This will save you lots of time and energy. When dining out with baby, all you'll have to do is add a fresh bottle or fresh food or both.

When baby is small (before he sits up unassisted), take along to the restaurant:

❦ An infant seat or stroller

❦ An extra bottle of formula or juice

❦ Disposable diapers with a plastic trash bag (for dirty diapers)

❦ Wipes and tissues

❦ A cloth diaper (for burping)

❦ A bib

❦ One or two pacifiers (if baby uses them)

❦ A change of clothing

❦ An extra sweater or sweatshirt (restaurants tend to be cool)

❦ A few favorite toys

❦ Receiving blanket to cover baby

Once your child is sitting up unassisted, call the restaurant ahead of time to be sure it has sturdy high chairs available. Chances are, if they don't have high chairs, they don't encourage young families to dine there. In addition to the items listed above, here's what you'll need for the older baby and toddler:

❦ Baby's favorite prepared food, packed in baby jars or tightly sealed plastic containers (finger foods can be cut in advance and placed in airtight sealed plastic sandwich bags)

❦ Rubber-coated baby spoon

❦ An empty training cup

❋ A few favorite toys

❋ A few books (cloth or sturdy cardboard)

❋ A teething biscuit to keep him busy

Time-Tested Advice

❦ To help a young baby stay quiet and settled down in a restaurant, keep him in a baby carrier.

❦ To keep your child from getting bored, don't give him food, toys, and books all at the same time. Dole them out as you go from one course to another.

❦ If the service is slow, take turns walking or strolling your child outside the restaurant.

❦ Take the opportunity of eating out to begin teaching your toddler how to behave considerately in public places.

❦ Don't allow your child to run around the restaurant. It's not only impolite to others, it's unsafe.

❧ 12 ❧

S.O.S.: *Safety Tips*

You can never over-childproof your home. It's up to you to protect baby against all potential hazards. For her sake and yours, plan ahead. Begin by touring your home on your hands and knees. You'll get a whole different perspective on the dangers that can attract your curious child's attention.

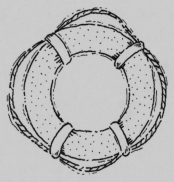

It's best to remove any precious and fragile items that might be tempting to little fingers. When childproofing your home, keep in mind that baby's movements develop in stages from crawling to standing to walking to climbing. If you do a thoughtful and comprehensive job, your reward will be fewer *no*'s and a safer household. As your toddler gets older, she will imitate her role model—you! That's why it's important to practice what you preach about safety.

All items discussed below can be found at local children's specialty shops, hardware stores, drugstores, five and dime stores, department stores, and discount warehouses. To save time and energy, call ahead and check to see if the stores have them in stock.

Baby Equipment Safety Information

Besides providing you with a list of the basic equipment you'll need for baby from birth to toddlerhood, this section also includes safety tips for proper usage. Remember, all baby equipment must meet the Consumer Product Safety Commission's standards. Always check for its seal of approval before you buy.

Car Seat

PINK AND BLUE ALERT

Never travel with your child on your lap!

You must always put your child in a car seat—even if it's just to go around the block. (For detailed information on choice of seats and placement in the car, see Chapter 6, "Home from the Hospital.") Both the American Academy of Pediatrics and your local police department advocate the use of a car seat, so please pay careful attention to the following information!

PINK AND BLUE HINT

Use soft toys for baby's traveling entertainment, particularly those that can be safely attached to the seat. No long cords! It's also nice to play music for baby in the car.

☀ Before purchasing baby's car seat, make sure that your particular choice will fit into your car, with your seat belts.

☀ Always follow the manufacturer's directions for installation. Use all the parts included with the seat. Check the seat before putting baby into it to be sure straps and bolts are secured correctly.

☀ Make sure baby is sitting in car seat at appropriate angle for her body weight. When she's properly secured and the seat is adjusted for her, you're ready to go.

❀ On hot days, cover the car seat with a towel or blanket so exposed metal or plastic parts of the seat won't burn baby's skin.

❀ If you need to comfort a crying baby, pull over to the side of the road. Never remove a child from her seat while the car is in motion.

❀ Don't feed your child while driving. You can't watch baby and keep your eyes on the road at the same time.

❀ If your car seat is vinyl, purchase washable cloth car seat covers. These will be more comfortable for baby!

❀ If your toddler resists sitting in the car seat and weighs forty pounds or more, you can use a booster car seat that requires seat belt restraint.

PINK AND BLUE ALERT

Never leave a child alone in the car—not even for a second!

PINK AND BLUE HINT

Be a good model for your children and always wear a seat belt. Make a rule for the young child—no car seat, no seat belt, *no ride!*

Carriage

A carriage is a luxury item and should be used only for the first eight weeks. If you can borrow one from a friend or relative, do so. It can also double as a bassinet. Due to the bulkiness of a carriage, it isn't quite as portable as a stroller. A carriage should have:

❀ Secure locking brakes

❀ Well-padded interior

❀ No protruding metal parts

❀ Easy mobility (should glide without effort)

❀ Ability to fold for storage

High Chair

When your baby can sit in an upright position unassisted, she is old enough to sit in a high chair. This usually occurs

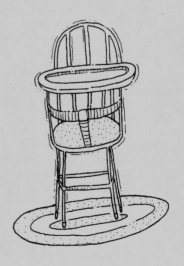

PINK AND BLUE HINT

Use a dish with a suction cup so baby can't throw it on the floor. Place a large plastic tarp under the high chair for easy cleanup.

around six months old when you begin introducing solid foods. Before you seat her in the high chair, have her food ready, along with a bib, utensils, and bottle or cup. Never leave baby alone or unattended in the high chair. If you forget something, take baby with you. Here are some other safety rules to follow at mealtime:

- ✤ Make sure you use the seat belt to secure the child in the high chair so she doesn't slip or slide out.

- ✤ The food tray must be locked on both sides. Watch out for baby's fingers as you lock and unlock the tray.

- ✤ Always clean the tray well after each feeding. Baby can't discern between fresh food and old, spoiled food.

- ✤ If your high chair is the folding type, always make sure it's securely locked.

- ✤ Don't allow baby to stand or climb in or out of the high chair.

- ✤ Place the high chair in a safe open area, away from tables or walls that baby can push against and allow the high chair to tip over.

- ✤ While an antique high chair is lovely, it is not advisable unless the base is steady and the chair has a proper seat strap.

- ✤ For a wooden high chair, it's a good idea to use a soft, wipeable cushion for the seat and back.

- ✤ Don't encourage toys at meal times. It's hard enough for baby to concentrate on food!

- ✤ Occasionally check the sturdiness of the high chair (tighten screws, glides on legs, tray latch).

Infant Seat

Infant seats are handy for carrying babies. Be sure the one you choose is sturdy and has a wide bottom base. The following precautions are very important:

❧ Never leave baby unattended in an infant seat.

❧ Always strap baby into the seat.

❧ Never use an infant seat in place of an approved car seat.

❧ Place the infant seat on the floor instead of on a table, chair, or countertop. Baby can rock the seat and fall off.

Playpen

You can utilize a playpen when baby is three months old. Two types are available: wooden and mesh. While the wooden playpen makes it easier for baby to pull up to a standing position, the mesh is softer for cushioning falls. Ask your pediatrician which type she recommends. Here are some safety guidelines to keep in mind for either choice:

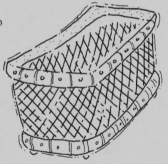

❧ Wooden playpen slats must be no more than 2⅜ inches apart.

❧ If playpen is painted, the paint must be lead-free.

❧ The netting on mesh playpens must be very fine, so the mesh doesn't catch on clothing buttons and little fingers can't stick through.

❧ All metal parts must be well-padded and covered.

❧ The sides of the playpen must always be securely locked in place. Recheck the locking mechanism to be absolutely certain that it won't collapse and that little fingers won't get caught. (Periodically check for loose screws, nuts, and bolts.)

PINK AND BLUE HINT

While the family is eating dinner, strap baby in the infant seat and put her in the bassinet. Baby is now at eye level and can "participate" in the family meal.

PINK AND BLUE HINT

Don't overuse the playpen. Too much use gives baby a negative feeling about it. To keep her from getting bored, change the toys periodically.

PINK AND BLUE ALERT

It's very important to teach your toddler how to crawl up and down the stairs. On the bottom three steps, show child repeatedly how to crawl down backward.

※ Place a terry cloth cover over the vinyl pad. Keep an extra cover on hand so when one is dirty there's always a clean replacement. (The cover protects baby's skin from sticking to the vinyl coating.)

※ Keep the playpen in an area of the house where there is the most foot traffic. Baby will enjoy all the activity and you can keep an eye on her.

※ Baby should not be left unattended in the playpen; it is not meant to be a baby-sitter.

※ All toys placed in the playpen should be nontoxic and childproof. Avoid small toys that baby can put in her mouth and choke on. Stuffed animals with protruding facial features should either be watched very carefully or not put in the playpen.

Safety Gates

Install gates at the top and bottom of stairs as well as in doorways where you don't want baby to have access. Be sure to lock the gates on staircases securely so your child can't push the gate open and fall down the stairs. There are a variety of safety gate styles, each with different capabilities. They are available in plastic or wood. The approved choices are hardware mounted or pressure mounted, made of rigid plastic or wire mesh. Don't use old gates leftover from grandma or friends (this includes the accordion type).

Stroller

Invest in a good, sturdy stroller with excellent back support and reclining positions that can last from infancy through the toddler years. While the umbrella stroller type is less expensive, it provides little back support, has poor stability, and can tip over easily. Some guidelines to keep in mind are:

❖ Test ride a stroller before buying it!

❖ The stroller you purchase should have wheels that glide easily, a good brake, evenly distributed balance with a wide, non-tip base, and no protruding metal parts. You should be able to collapse it easily.

❖ If your stroller doesn't have a hood, attachable stroller umbrellas are available.

❖ If your stroller doesn't have a pouch for storage, you can buy one that slips onto the handles.

❖ When opening the stroller from a collapsed position, check and recheck the locking clip.

❖ Always use the seat belt straps!

❖ If your stroller is metal, don't forget to cover it with a beach towel or blanket when it is exposed to heat.

❖ Put your name on your stroller.

Walkers

While walkers are available, most pediatricians do not recommend them. They are dangerous and when overused can inhibit the development of crawling.

Childproofing Tips: Household Overview

Your home can be hazardous to baby's health and welfare if you don't do a thorough job of childproofing. Don't take anything for granted; use common sense. Begin by doing the following:

❖ Put safety plugs or safety covers on all electrical outlets. When possible, place furniture in front of outlets.

PINK AND BLUE HINT
Don't put too many items in the pouch because the stroller can tip over.

PINK AND BLUE HINT
Tie a toy to the stroller with a short string or ribbon. Baby can be happily occupied; the toy will not be lost and you won't have to constantly bend over to pick it up.

❋ Install childproof safety locks or latches on all cabinets and drawers that are accessible to baby.

❋ Lock up all medications, household cleaning products, aerosol cans, alcoholic beverages, and other dangerous substances and keep them out of a child's reach. Some of the dangerous (not all are poisonous) household products are: washing detergents, bleaches, abrasive cleaners, mothballs, glue, disinfectants, pet food, cosmetics, lye, insect repellents, and furniture polish. Always read label ingredients and look for the universal poison sign.

❋ Put plastic bags and metal hangers from dry cleaners and stores in covered garbage cans, out of your child's reach.

❋ Place felt appliqués on all sharp corners of furniture or buy baby-proof edge covers to wrap around coffee tables.

❋ Inside the house, be careful of doors with locks. Either remove the lock or have the key to that door available to you or any other adult in the home.

❋ For doors you don't want children to open, buy a special plastic door knob cover that must be squeezed to turn the knob. It's easy for adults but impossible for children.

❋ To keep your child inside the house, make sure you attach a hook and eye lock at an adult's height to all doors leading outside.

❋ On sliding glass doors, place a colorful decal at a child's eye level so she will know the glass is there.

❋ Since long cords are dangerous, either roll them up when not in use, replace them with shorter cords, or buy cord covers.

❋ Never leave an electrical cord dangling from a table or counter.

❦ Replace old, frayed electrical cords. They are fire hazards!

❦ Equip your home with smoke detectors and at least one fire extinguisher. Hang the extinguisher on a wall at an adult's height. Change the batteries in smoke detectors yearly.

❦ Be prepared for power failures. Have a few flashlights (with extra batteries) available in the kitchen and master bedroom (by your bedside). Also, stock your home with candles.

❦ Keep matches, lighters, and ashtrays out of a child's reach.

❦ All fireplaces should be covered with safe, heavy screens that a child can't move.

❦ If you have stairs in your house, gates should be placed at the top and bottom of the staircase (see Safety Gates, page 118). Wrap mesh netting (available at juvenile or safety stores) around the open posts of a staircase banister to prevent a child from slipping through. Or, if the netting is a decorative eyesore, attach Plexiglas to the banisters with bolts and screws so the posts are covered.

❦ Make sure all windows have screens and window locks. Children should not play near, or with, any open windows. If you have blinds on your windows, cut open the loop on cords and tie them or purchase cord covers because they can cause strangulation.

❦ Keep pet bowls out of reach of a mobile child.

❦ Make sure all area rugs have nonskid backings to prevent slipping accidents.

❦ If you own a gun and live ammunition, lock them in a closet or cabinet that your child cannot open.

PINK AND BLUE HINT

Store batteries in an accessible place. For longer life of a battery, place batteries in a closed container on the top shelf of your refrigerator.

❤ Place jewelry items in a box out of a child's reach. Things that are small, shiny, and glittery are very attractive and tempting.

❤ Keep sewing, knitting, crocheting, and needlepoint supplies out of a child's reach.

❤ When throwing away poisonous items, rinse out containers and dispose of them in outside covered garbage cans.

❤ At holiday time, be careful of small tree ornaments, Hanukkah coins, and dreidels that can cause choking. In addition, hang decorative lights high and out of baby's grasp.

❤ If you're concerned about carbon monoxide, purchase a carbon monoxide detector at your local hardware or safety store.

Time-Tested Household Safety Advice

❤ Never carry baby while drinking a hot beverage. She can be burned easily.

❤ Never allow your child to eat while walking, running, lying down, or sitting in a moving car. Be especially careful of foods on sticks, such as lollipops and Popsicles.

❤ Never allow toys or playing on the staircase.

❤ Keep your child away from all trash cans.

❤ Never leave your child alone by a lit fireplace.

❤ Keep your child away from fans, electric wall heaters, floor heaters, and radiators.

- Never leave your child alone with a pet. You can't hold an animal accountable for its behavior.

- Don't allow young children to blow up balloons or put balloons in their mouths. They can cause choking. (For toy safety, see Chapter 13, "Activities, Books, Music, and Toys.")

Childproofing Tips: Room by Room

Here is a room-by-room checklist to further protect your child.

Bathroom

- Lock up all medicines (including vitamins)!

- Check the dates on medications and throw out all expired medicines.

- Keep powders, soaps, colognes, shaving items (razors and blades), and all other toiletries locked up and out of reach.

- Buy protective spout and knob covers to prevent burns and bumping.

- Make sure the bathtub has a bath mat, nonskid strips, or appliqués.

- Keep the toilet bowl lid closed and locked at all times; purchase toilet seat safety locks. A child can drown in a small amount of water. Open toilets are tempting to play in and very dangerous, not to mention unsanitary.

- Keep hair dryers unplugged and out of sight when not in use.

- Glass items in the bathroom are not safe. Use plastic cups and soap dishes (and plastic for any other vanity table items). For decorative purposes, you can purchase clear Lucite accessories.

❧ Syrup of ipecac should be stored in your medicine cabinet in case baby ingests medicines, household cleaners, or some poisonous item. If this occurs, always call poison control immediately for directions. *Never* induce vomiting unless so instructed.

Time-Tested Bathroom Safety Advice

❧ Never leave your child alone in the bathtub or bathroom. If the doorbell or telephone rings, don't answer it!

❧ Before bathing your child, test the bathwater temperature and always turn the hot water off first.

❧ Don't let baby play with the powder container because she can aspirate the powder and choke.

PINK AND BLUE HINT

When rearranging and childproofing your kitchen, select one accessible cabinet or drawer for your toddler. Store plastic containers of various sizes, unbreakable bowls, wooden spoons, and safe play toys in it. Your child can play along while you cook, but not too close to hot appliances. Try having a drawer or cabinet with things for your toddler in your office or master bedroom, too!

Kitchen

❧ Make sure utensil drawers holding sharp knives and forks have safety locks.

❧ Keep all electrical appliances out of reach to prevent toppling on your child. Cords, push buttons, and bright colors attract a child's attention.

❧ Keep doors closed on your washer and dryer. Children shouldn't be able to climb into them or turn them on.

❧ Beware of tablecloths that may be tempting for a toddler to pull. If there are items on the cloth (hot cup of coffee, heavy dish, planter, vase, or lamp), they'll fall on your child.

☀ If trash can is reachable, be sure to have a securely closed lid. It's best to keep trash cans out of reach.

Time-Tested Kitchen Safety Advice

☀ While cooking, make sure pot's and pan's handles are turned toward the back of the stove. Fry and boil on back burners.

☀ Remember to keep baby away from hot appliances such as the stove, oven, and iron. Some hardware, juvenile, or safety stores carry stove knob covers and oven locks.

☀ When removing hot dishes from the stove, oven, or microwave, keep children away and set dishes out of reach.

☀ Wrap all sharp objects, such as tin can lids, before throwing them in the garbage.

☀ Quickly wipe up spills before your child or anyone can slip.

☀ Clean up broken glass with a broom or vacuum cleaner; then follow with damp towels.

Outdoors

☀ If there is a swimming pool or spa in your backyard, it must be safely enclosed with a fence and gate and locked securely at all times!

PINK AND BLUE ALERT

Even if your baby takes swimming lessons, she is not pool safe. Never leave her alone in a pool!

☀ When baby is in a swimming pool, the inflatable arm bands and inflatable tubes are only extra precautionary measures. They are not substitutes for careful adult supervision.

☀ If you keep tools in the garage or shed, store them out of your child's reach. It's best to keep tools locked up in a separate container. Toddlers are fascinated by these objects and can be quite creative in climbing to reach them.

☀ Outdoor gardening products should be stored out of your child's reach because many are poisonous. Included in this category are weed killers, snail poisons, and fertilizers.

☀ Car maintenance products, such as oil, gasoline, and brake and cleaning fluids, should be stored high above a child's reach.

☀ If you are storing an unused refrigerator or freezer, put a lock on the doors, remove them, or better yet, get rid of the appliance.

☀ Make sure your backyard (outdoor) play equipment is safe for your toddler.

☀ If you have a balcony, deck, or terrace, use mesh netting or Plexiglas to cover guard railings, and never leave child unattended.

Time-Tested Outdoor Safety Advice

❀ Don't leave a baby or toddler alone outside. There must be constant adult supervision.

- Keep your child away from lawn mowers and other gardening equipment. If your child is in the garden with you, give her a plastic toy gardening set.

- Keep young children away from hot barbecue grills. Never hold baby while you cook.

- Visits to the park should be carefully monitored. Watch out for broken glass, beer cans, and dog excrement.

- Check playground equipment before allowing your toddler to play (look for splinters, broken or wet steps, exposed nails, and rusty metal parts). Teach your toddler not to run in front of other children on swings and slides.

- When crossing the street, either carry your child or hold her hand tightly.

- When using gardening or car maintenance products, be careful to keep them away from your child.

Plants

Pretty colors and soft, smooth items immediately attract baby's attention. She wants to touch and she wants to taste. But beware, she's not selective about what goes into her mouth! That's why you must remove all poisonous plants from baby's reach. Also label all indoor plants by their botanical name. Should baby eat a leaf, you'll be able to quickly identify it for your doctor or poison control center.

The Los Angeles County Arboretum has compiled a partial list of poisonous plants to serve as a guideline. These are:

angel's trumpet	autumn crocus	baneberry
azaleas	bleeding hearts	boxwoods
bushman's poison	caladiums	carolina jasmine
castor bean	chinaberry tree	coral plant
crown thorns	daffodils	daphnes
delphiniums	dumbcanes (diffenbochis)	elderberries
elephant's ears	English laurel	false hellebores
vicia faba	foxglove	glory lily
hemp	hollies	horse chestnuts
hyacinths and bulbs	hydrangea	ivies
jimson weed	jamestown weed	lantanas
lily of the valley	locust	mescal bean
milk bush	mistletoe	monk shoals
narcissus bulbs	night-blooming jasmine	nutmeg
oaks	oleander	philodendrons
poinsettia	pokeweed	privets
rattlebox	rhododendrons	rosary pea
skyflowers	sweet pea	tomato plant leaves
Virginia creeper	water hemlock	wisterias
yellow oleander	yews	

Consult your pediatrician, poison control center, and local Department of Parks and Recreation for additional names of harmful plants.

Emergency Information

Emergency telephone numbers, addresses, and vital information should always be posted by at least one phone in the house, preferably in the kitchen. The list should include:

※ Father's and mother's work

※ Pediatrician

※ Neighbor

※ Relative

※ Police (911)

※ Fire and paramedics (911)

※ Poison control center

※ Local hospital emergency room

※ Pharmacy

※ Children's names and birth dates

※ Home address, phone number, and name of nearest cross street

You should always leave a letter of consent and authorization with the baby-sitter or caretaker responsible for your child in your absence. This letter authorizes the caretaker to get medical treatment for your child in your absence, if necessary. If you're going away for an extended period of time or if you're going out of the country, the letter must be notarized. Also prepare a consent letter for your pediatrician.

If there are any special instructions (such as medications to take) or known allergies, leave this information in writing. When you're going out, always leave a phone number where you can be reached in case of an emergency. If you're unreachable, call home frequently or carry a beeper. Anyone baby-sitting your child should know infant CPR (cardiopulmonary resuscitation). Classes are offered by some physicians, hospitals, the local YMCA, or Red Cross.

꧁ 13 ꧁

Activities, Books,
Music, and Toys

You've brought a new little person into this world, and from the moment he arrives, he's going to be learning about himself and the world he lives in. It's up to you to help stimulate his senses and develop his mind. Your baby's brain is like a sponge, and you'll delight in seeing how much he absorbs. By selecting appropriate activities, books, music, and toys, you will cultivate your child's curiosity, foster his imagination, and develop his self-confidence.

Activities

Once your child is four to six months old, you may want to join a play group. At first, this will serve primarily as a social experience for you to meet other parents with children of the same age and to share and exchange ideas. As baby develops, he will learn to recognize his playmates and enjoy being around familiar faces.

Call your local YMCA, park and recreation department, pediatrician, hospital, religious institution, or neighborhood nursery school to find out what type of Parent and Baby or Toddler classes are offered in your area. If you can't find a suitable program, organize your own play group with friends who have babies of the same age, or with parents from your birthing classes. You may also want to enroll your baby or toddler in a children's gym class where both parent and child participate together. Doing any activity with your child is an excellent beginning of your child's social awareness, as well as a continuation of parent and child bonding.

Activities Outside the Home

Taking your child outside the home to see the world around him is very important. Even a change of scenery, such as your own backyard, is exciting to him. What we as adults take for granted takes on a whole new dimension when seen through the eyes of a young child. Don't be afraid to explore new and different places with him. Some suggestions for these activities are:

※ Picnic in your own backyard (sing songs, read a book)

※ Garden with your child

※ Walk your child in his stroller (around the neighborhood, at the park, through a shopping mall)

※ For the confident little walker, hold his hand and take a short walk (around the block or through the park)

※ Go to a local playground or park where there is age-appropriate equipment, such as swings and slides

❧ Visit the zoo (or look for a petting zoo)

❧ Visit a pet store

❧ Go to a children's museum

❧ Go to an aquarium

Arts and Crafts Activities

When your child is eighteen months or older, there are a wide variety of arts and crafts activities you can share with him at home. All these activities are also great to do with a small play group. Whether with one child or several, adult supervision is required at all times. It's a practical necessity to have a change of clothing for each child. To complete the play group day, don't forget to include a nutritious snack and drink.

Here are some arts and crafts activity suggestions:

❧ Coloring with jumbo nontoxic crayons and paper

❧ Play dough with accessories (rolling pin, plastic cookie cutters, garlic press)

❧ Finger painting (make sure the child wears a smock or an adult's old shirt)

❧ Using nontoxic paste, paste different shapes and textures of paper or magazine pictures onto construction paper

❧ Vegetable and sponge painting (cut a potato, carrot, turnip, or sponge into a shape, dip in tempera paint, apply to paper)

PINK AND BLUE HINT

Put a large piece of paper on an easel, or tape paper to the floor or table to make it easier for children to color. Use masking tape.

PINK AND BLUE HINT

Make your own play dough with the following recipe: 1 cup flour, 1 cup water, 1/2 cup salt, 1 teaspoon cream of tartar, 1 tablespoon oil, food coloring (ten to twenty drops, depending on degree of color you want). Mix all ingredients and cook over medium heat until mixture pulls away from sides of pan and becomes very thick in consistency. Knead until cool. Keeps three months in an airtight container or sealed plastic bag at room temperature.

☀ Water play (depending on the weather, a good outdoor activity)

☀ Sand play (another good outdoor activity, using plastic pails, shovels, molds, strainers, trucks, and cars)

☀ Rice or pasta play (Fill large shallow box or container with uncooked rice, noodles, or curly pasta. Never leave child unattended; be sure he doesn't eat the uncooked food!)

☀ Various-sized cardboard boxes (children love to climb and explore in and out of *open* containers)

☀ Role playing (children love to dress up in grown-up clothing with hats, shirts, stoles, and gloves, and do household chores such as dusting, sweeping, and make-believe cooking)

Books

Studies indicate that exposing your child to reading materials at a very young age is beneficial. Not only does this familiarize your child with the idea of reading, but it contributes to his intellectual and emotional growth as well. The children's book market is filled with different types of books covering a variety of topics. Your baby's first books might include any of the following:

Board books are sturdy, wear-resistant, and have wipeable pages of durable cardboard. They have colorful, striking illustrations designed to attract and hold baby's attention. Topics you can choose from are animals, toys, transportation, occupations, numbers, alphabet, colors, shapes, food, and family.

Touch and feel books enhance the tactile experience. There is a good variety to select from, featuring familiar items in the child's environment.

Peek-a-boo books are filled with fun surprises for the very young child. Doors open, flaps lift, and parts move as the toddler discovers hidden objects.

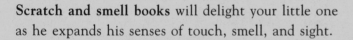

Interactive books encourage manipulative participation by the child. Included in these books are finger puppets, flaps, cutouts, and die-cut holes.

Scratch and smell books will delight your little one as he expands his senses of touch, smell, and sight.

Bath time books are foam-filled, vinyl coated, safe, soft, and nontoxic. These colorful, floatable books will help every child enjoy bath time!

Picture books tell entire stories through bold, well-illustrated pictures. These are collectibles for your child's future library.

Here are some perennial favorites:

A to Z by Sandra Boynton, Little Simon

Babar's Bath Book by Laurent DeBrunhoff, Random House

Best First Book Ever! by Richard Scarry, Random House

Goodnight Moon by Margaret Wise Brown, HarperCollins

Pat the Bunny by Dorothy Kunhardt, Western Publishing (A Golden Book)

The Very Hungry Caterpillar by Eric Carle, Philomel Books

Where's Spot? by Eric Hill, Putnam (all "Spot" books)

For additional help in selecting literature for your child, see:

The Read-Aloud Handbook by Jim Trelease, Penguin Books

Hey Listen to This by Jim Trelease, Penguin Books

For Reading Out Loud! by Margaret Mary Kimmel and Elizabeth Segal, Delacorte Press

I'll Tell You a Story, I'll Sing You a Song by Christine Allsion, Childcare Books

Raising Readers: A Guide to Sharing Literature with Young Children by Linda Leonard Lamme, Vivian Cox, Jane Matanzo, Mike Olson, Walker and Co.

Let's Read Together by Let's Read Together Revision Committee Association for Library Service to Children, American Library Association

Music

PINK AND BLUE HINT

Make your own cassette tape of your child's favorite collection of

Music is an integral part of all of our lives, and appreciation of music can begin at infancy. Lullabies and classical music provide soothing moments for you and your child. They also promote peaceful solitary play.

A wide selection of children's music is available in cassette and compact disc form. Old favorites such as nursery rhymes and narrated stories flourish in the recorded music market. Other popular recordings provide delightful activities like dance, sing-alongs, finger play, and rhythm play (with and without children using instruments), along with simple instructions. Some wonderful selections include music by the following well-known children's recording artists:

Marcia Berman

Bethie

Tom Glazer

Greg and Steve

Burl Ives

Ella Jenkins

Hap Palmer

Peter, Paul, and Mary

Raffi

Rosenshontz

Pete Seeger

Sharon, Lois, and Bram

Sweet Honey and the Rock

Most of the music described above can be purchased at local record outlets, children's specialty and toy shops, department stores, and discount stores. You can also borrow cassettes and albums from your local library, school, or religious institution.

Toys

When selecting toys for your baby, first make sure the toys are safe. Inspect toys before buying them. If possible, purchase unopened, sealed toys. Choose toys that develop hand-eye coordination, promote fine and gross motor skills, encourage decision-making, and foster creativity. Buy toys that are geared to your child's age, development, and ability. When shopping in a toy store, keep in mind that the toy is for your child, not for you.

Age-Appropriate Toys: Birth to One Year

Since infants spend most of their energy eating and sleeping, it's not necessary to spend a lot of money on toys for newborns. There are a few crib toys that are a good source of entertainment, but only for the first five months. After that, they must be removed because baby begins reaching for objects, and these toys can fall on him.

- ❀ A **musical mobile** in bright colors stimulates baby's senses by the time he's approximately four weeks old. Hang the mobile in the crib, but not directly over baby's head. (Remove at five months.)

- ❀ A **crib gym** encourages hand-eye coordination. Be sure the crib gym is not too difficult to grasp; the slightest touch should quickly offer a positive response. This toy is best suited for a three- to five-month-old baby, or until baby can push himself up on his hands and knees. (Remove at five months.)

- ❀ An **activity center** should be securely and safely mounted on the crib slats. In addition to providing entertainment, it encourages a variety of skills. Several manufacturers have created soft, cloth activity centers for the parent who is concerned about the plastic models. There's nothing like awakening to the sound of a bell or a winding clock; it's delightful to hear your baby amusing himself! (Remove at five months.)

- ❀ A **crib mirror** is safe and fun for baby. The reflection is not distorted, even though the mirror isn't made of glass. Seeing a face with various expressions is stimulating. (Remove at five months.)

- A **rattle** develops grasping and visual skills. Make sure it's constructed in one piece and is large enough so it won't get stuck in baby's throat.

- **Stuffed animals** and **rag dolls** are two basic items children love to cuddle and touch. That's why they're typical gift items. However, don't overcrowd the crib or playpen with too many. Make sure there are no protruding or removable parts on these toys.

- **Textured toys** quietly stimulate baby's sense of touch. A baby likes to explore the variety of textures presented to him, such as fake fur, flannel, vinyl, cut velvet, plain cotton, or terry cloth.

- **Balls** are always a source of enjoyment regardless of your child's age or gender. A rubber ball with indentations that baby can easily grasp provides instant gratification. Clear plastic roll-and-float balls enchant the child on the floor, as well as in the bathtub.

- **Squeeze and squeak toys** are great fun for baby to hear and touch.

- **Rubber or plastic rings** are easy-to-grasp toys for baby that are also great for teething.

- **Toys with suction cups** can be set on a hard-surface floor or high chair tray. The easy play and bounce-back motion of such toys thrill the child and, at the same time, encourage manual dexterity and hand-eye coordination.

- Large (three to four inches in diameter) **colorful plastic blocks** that baby can hold and stack with both hands continue to develop hand-eye coordination.

PINK AND BLUE HINT

Textured toys can be purchased in block, doll, animal, or book form. Or be creative and make one of your own from scrap materials. Avoid rough textures for now—baby's skin is sensitive.

❉ **Peek-a-boo games** with your hands and baby's hands provide simple entertainment and positive interaction between baby and adult.

❉ Use **empty plastic containers** for baby to learn how to grasp objects and the concept of putting in and taking out.

Age-Appropriate Toys: One Year to Eighteen Months

This is an exciting time in your child's life. He's mastering the "fine art" of walking and is continually developing mentally and physically. There are many toys and games available to promote your child's development. Keep in mind that your young child's attention span is short and he can be easily distracted, which is perfectly normal and age-appropriate.

❉ **Stacking cubes** in a variety of primary colors and sizes are great for grasping and can keep baby occupied while sitting and playing. They also help teach the concept of building and toppling.

❉ **Push and pull toys** help develop walking skills. Pull toys are available in an assortment of sizes and types, including wagons, animals, cars, planes, trucks, and trains. Children love colorful pull toys that make noise. This will be helpful to you in locating your child anywhere in the house! Be sure the cord on the pull toy is no longer than six to eight inches. Child-sized durable plastic shopping baskets, poppers, vacuum cleaners, carpet sweepers, and lawn mowers are all entertaining push toys.

❉ **Riding toys** must have equal balance, wide-base support, easy steering, and easy-to-grab handlebars. Make sure the riding toy you choose is well proportioned to your child's body size. If his feet don't reach the floor, then the toy is not the right size for him. Other features to consider are shape, color, storage compartment, and sound.

PINK AND BLUE ALERT

Until your child masters the riding toy, don't let him ride it on a hard concrete, brick, or stone surface.

☼ **Bath toys** allow your child to experiment with water by pouring and splashing. It's a great diversion for the child who resists taking a bath. Plastic toys such as boats, ducks, and fish demonstrate floating. More elaborate bath toys hook to the side of the tub and stimulate water play with items that slide, spin, and spout (see Chapter 12, "S.O.S.: Safety Tips," and Time-Tested Bathroom Safety Advice on page 124).

☼ **Surprise boxes** create an immediate positive response when the child pushes, dials, or pulls the appropriate switches or buttons. Your child will delight in the pop-up figure that he activates.

☼ **Shape sorters** teach the child to recognize shapes and differentiate one from another by trial and error. The child learns to put the correct shape into its corresponding cut-out, and memory skills are introduced.

☼ **Telephones** are fun for your child because he loves to imitate mom and dad. As your child gets older, the play telephone creatively inspires make-believe conversations while cultivating imagination and fluency of speech.

Age-Appropriate Toys: Eighteen Months to Two Years

At this age, your child is extremely mobile, curious, and just beginning to become social. It's important to have a variety of toys to occupy and stimulate his active mind. It's a good idea to rotate your child's toys to arouse his interests and keep him from getting bored with them.

☼ **Hammering toys** release frustration and anger and provide the opportunity to make loud, gratifying noises. These toys encourage hand-eye coordination. An adult should supervise this activity to ensure that the hammer is being used properly.

PINK AND BLUE ALERT

Choke test tubes are available at toy or safety stores. If a toy or object fits through this tube, then it is too small for baby and can cause choking.

❦ Large, colorful **interlocking blocks** that snap together help cultivate your child's fine and gross motor skills. They also develop creativity.

❦ **Small wooden or plastic blocks** with letters, numbers, or popular cartoon characters reinforce fine motor skills and dexterity.

❦ **Cardboard brick blocks** are light and easy for your toddler to handle. They are inexpensive, durable, safe, and quiet. (At this age, large wooden blocks are too heavy and dangerous for your child to manipulate.) Since these blocks are all the same size, your toddler's attempts at building are uncomplicated and provide quick, satisfying results.

❦ The **tapered cone with multicolored rings** which graduate in size teaches the concepts of large and small, as well as stacking and building. These plastic rings are well suited for this age range, because the teething toddler has a tendency to chew on them!

❦ **Plastic or fabric dolls** are safest for your toddler. They encourage role-playing and imagination. It's not wise to purchase accessories for dolls. Porcelain or any fragile doll should not be given to a toddler.

❦ **Puzzles** for toddlers are excellent for hand-eye coordination and perceptual discrimination. Look for puzzles with four or five large pieces that are colorful and easy to manipulate. Some manufacturers have an easy-lift knob in the center of each piece, with a surprise picture under that puzzle part.

❦ A **pail and shovel** can entertain your child for an indefinite amount of time. Many sets come with rakes, molds, and strainers. The idea of playing in the sand or dirt and being allowed to make a mess is very exciting for your child.

❋ **Riding toys** can now include a tricycle, as well as the animal and car toys mentioned under *One Year to Eighteen Months*. These children's vehicles should be well proportioned to your child's body size and weight. When purchasing this item, take into consideration equal balance, easy steering, and well-padded handlebars.

❋ **Play or modeling dough** is a wonderful material that always stimulates creativity and entertains the toddler. He can pound, poke, touch, and pull the soft dough and receive an immediate sense of accomplishment. Rolling the dough and cutting out shapes never gets boring!

❋ The **toy playhouse, farm, garage, airport, school, or hospital** with accompanying plastic figures and accessories is a great diversion for your child. The little plastic people sit in their appropriate environment and are easy for the child to manipulate. This is one toy that doesn't require much adult interaction and can be entertaining for hours. The toddler's imagination will run wild with this toy.

❋ The **indoor gym**, preferably made of sturdy plastic, will be one item your child will use for years. It encourages the gross motor skills of climbing and sliding. You can set it up inside your home or, when the weather is warm, outside. You'll be amazed at the things your child will discover he can do on this piece of equipment. Adult supervision is imperative!

❋ A **child-sized playhouse** is lots of fun at this age. A sturdy plastic house is preferable to a wooden one because it doesn't splinter or weather (especially if you store it outside) and is easy to wipe clean after play. Children's cleaning utensils are fun and natural accessories to the

- Always check wooden toys for splinters; if necessary, sand them.
- Toys should not have cords or strings longer than eight inches. If the cord is longer, shorten or remove it.
- If you have older children, keep their toys (such as marbles, coins, tiny building blocks, and doll accessories) out of baby's reach.
- A young child should not blow up a balloon, play with an uninflated balloon, or play with broken pieces of a balloon. He can easily choke.
- Don't let your child play with plastic wrap or any interior packing material when opening new toys or gifts. Suffocation or inhalation can occur.
- Loud-sounding toys can not only scare a young child, but also can be harmful to his hearing.
- When a toddler is through playing with his toys, put them away

immediately. He may think he can use the toy as a step stool to climb to other objects out of his reach.

- Be careful how you store your child's toys (see Chapter 12, "S.O.S.: Safety Tips").

- A rattle should be constructed in one piece and be large enough to prevent it from lodging in baby's throat.

- Be careful of putting toys with sharp edges, metal winders, buttons, and any protruding parts in the crib. They are not recommended for the crib or unattended playpen.

- Crib toys that fasten on the two side rails should be removed when baby is five months old.

- Mobiles should not hang directly over baby's head and should be removed when he's five months old.

- Carefully follow toy manufacturers' assembly instructions.

Time-Tested Advice

- ❤ Buy age-appropriate toys for your child. Check labels on the package. If a toy is too easy, your child will get bored; if it's too difficult, he'll get frustrated and have a sense of failure.

- ❤ It's best to purchase toys that can be washed or wiped off to keep germs to a minimum.

- ❤ Purchase brightly colored toys that encourage baby's senses of touching, smelling, seeing, and hearing.

- ❤ Teach your toddler to take care of his toys.

- ❤ Teach your child responsible play behavior. Never allow him to throw a toy or hit anyone with it.

- ❤ Instead of always saying *no* when your child grabs something dangerous, distract him by giving him a toy.

house. Both little boys and girls love this make-believe play.

- ☀ If you have space available in your child's bedroom, or even in a den or family room, **child-sized table and chairs** are worth investing in. The comfort and perfect proportion of playing at his own table invites and encourages the toddler to play.

- ☀ A **kitchen set** with pots, pans, bowls, and spoons will encourage role modeling. Leave one cabinet available for toddler's kitchen supplies and toys. Some sets also come with plastic foods. Just make sure your child understands this is make-believe food! You can also give your child one or two of your pots, pans, and wooden spoons to play with.

Toy Organizers

To keep toys from being strewn all over your house, it's a good idea to store them safely when your child is not playing with them. This will prevent accidents and lost toys. Here are a few storage suggestions:

❋ Stackable plastic bins (with or without rollers)

❋ Large, plastic containers with lids

❋ Shallow toy chests (see Chapter 12, "S.O.S.: Safety Tips")

❋ Sturdy open shelves (only one or two, low enough for a child to reach)

❋ Wire mesh baskets (great at the bottom of a closet)

❋ Baskets with handles

ⓖ 14 ⓖ

Traveling

As a new parent, taking your baby anywhere seems like a major production. Each time you leave your house, you're loaded down with a diaper bag, equipment, and of course, baby. What you really need is a moving van, not a car! The good news is, with careful planning and thoughtful organization, you can become a pro at traveling, just as you will at everything else you do for baby. Whether you're taking baby to run errands, on a plane trip, or on a visit to grandma's, your motto should be "plan ahead."

Errands and Short Trips

To make life easier, try to plan your errands and short trips around your child's feeding and napping schedule. If the short trips are frequently to the same location, such as a grandparent's or relative's home, then leave the most commonly used items (diapers, diaper wipes, powder, clothing, empty bottles, a blanket sleeping bag, a few favorite toys) at that place. To be well prepared for these excursions, you should also pack the necessary items in your diaper bag and purse.

Packing Your Diaper Bag

Your diaper bag is your ever-ready resource for baby whenever you take her for an outing. A practical diaper bag should be plastic-lined and lightweight and have outside pockets for last-minute items. It should also have a sturdy shoulder strap. When you pack your diaper bag, make sure it contains:

- Disposable diapers and small garbage bags with ties for dirty diapers

- Powder

- Diaper rash ointment

- Petroleum jelly

- Diaper wipes and tissues

- A bottle of formula (if bottle-feeding) with protective nipple cover

- A bottle of juice (for six months and older) with protective nipple cover

- One or two extra nipples and nipple covers

- A tightly sealed jar of baby food and spoon (for six months and older—short trips only)

- Finger food packed in an airtight plastic bag (for ten months and older—short trips only)

- A bib

- A few pacifiers (if baby uses them)

- A complete change of clothing for baby

- A cloth diaper

- A sweater or jacket and hat (depending on your local climate)

- A lightweight blanket (can be used to cover car seat on a hot day or when changing baby in the car or on an unprotected surface)

- A few toys and books

- Hypoallergenic sunscreen

Packing Your Purse

Besides the usual personal items you carry in your purse, when going out with baby, take along your pediatrician's phone number. If you're going out-of-town for the day (or

Time-Tested Advice

One of the most common errands you'll do with baby is shopping at the grocery store or local mall. To make your outing easier and more pleasurable, try the following:

- If baby is small (fifteen to eighteen pounds), carry her in a front-positioned soft baby carrier while you shop.

- As baby gets larger, if you still want to carry her while you shop, try a baby backpack.

- Once baby sits up unassisted, you can purchase a special comfort cushion seat with an attached

PINK AND BLUE HINT

If your errand or short trip is going to be longer than one hour, store some formula in a small, well-insulated thermos container. When you're ready to feed baby, pour the formula into a clean, empty bottle. (If you're concerned about spills, take along a small funnel.)

PINK AND BLUE HINT

The purse pouch that clasps at the waistline, or fanny pack, is wonderful for the parent who wants free hands for holding baby and carrying a diaper bag.

PINK AND BLUE HINT

Once baby can munch on something by herself, bring a favorite food treat to occupy her while you shop. Don't leave her alone while she's eating; there's always a chance she may choke.

PINK AND BLUE ALERT

Don't leave your child unattended at any time in a store or car. With all the media coverage of child kidnapping, we all know how dangerous this can be. You must prevent your child from being another statistic.

strap and buckle that fits securely into the child section of the shopping cart, or you can buy a strap that buckles the child safely into the shopping cart seat. (Some markets already provide safety straps built into the child section of their shopping carts. Call ahead and inquire.)

❀ Don't put grocery bags close to baby's reach in the shopping cart or in the car.

❀ Store baby's stroller in the trunk of your car so it'll be easily accessible for shopping in a mall or on the street.

longer), be sure to ask your doctor for the phone number of a local pediatrician. Any specific medication baby is currently taking should be carried in your purse, not the diaper bag. It's also a good idea to have a small packet of tissues.

Long Trips

Those spur-of-the-moment trips you used to take before having children were exciting and terrific. While you can't be quite so spontaneous now, with advance preparation you can enjoy traveling with baby. Once you get the knack of it, you won't be so hesitant to take her along. But don't plan complex itineraries where every minute is scheduled. You need to be flexible when traveling with young children. Whether you're staying at someone's home or a motel or hotel, the first twenty-four hours may be an adjustment for you and your child. That's why it's important to take along the essentials for taking care of baby, as well as items that will comfort and entertain her. The key to a successful trip is careful planning and well-packed suitcases.

Packing Your Suitcase

If possible, begin packing a few days prior to your departure. As you think of things, set them aside. Besides what you pack for yourself, the following items should be included in your suitcase:

- A sufficient change of clothing for baby (appropriate for the climate)

- Extra supply of baby's toiletries (soap, shampoo, powder, diaper wipes, petroleum jelly, diaper rash emollient, cotton tip applicators, moisturizing cream, brush and comb, scissors or soft emery board)

- Plenty of disposable diapers

- A package of safety plugs for exposed electrical outlets

- A night light that plugs into an electrical outlet

- A travel clock

- A flashlight and extra batteries

- A thermometer

- Infant acetaminophen drops

- Inflatable tub (for small babies)

- Two or three large waterproof lap pads

- A few extra cloth diapers

- Small box of baby's laundry detergent

- Extra bottles, nipples, caps, covers, and bottle brush

- A few large plastic bags for dirty laundry

PINK AND BLUE HINT

Remove the shrink wrap from disposable diapers, and pack them around the edges of the suitcase. This saves space, and breakable items can be protected and cushioned by the diapers.

PINK AND BLUE HINT

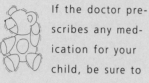

If the doctor prescribes any medication for your child, be sure to pack it in your purse. In case of accidental spills or lost medicine, ask your doctor for an extra written prescription.

PINK AND BLUE HINT

You can use your stroller in place of a high chair. Cover the seat with a large towel or sheet and strap baby in.

❀ Enough age-appropriate toys to alternate during trip (see Chapter 13, "Activities, Books, Music, and Toys")

Modes of Transportation

Time-Tested Advice

❤ When taking long trips with baby, you may want to plan travel times around her nap or bedtime schedule. If you're going to a different time zone, it's best to get you and baby adjusted to the new time immediately.

❤ It's a good idea for your child to have a checkup before you leave. (If any immunizations are required, plan your office visit well in advance, in case your child has reactions.)

❤ If you're planning to stay in a motel or hotel, be sure to book a room in advance.

❤ For each destination you're visiting, call ahead and see if you need to rent a crib, high chair, and playpen (optional).

❤ Make sure all baby equipment you rent is safe (see Chapter 12, "S.O.S.: Safety Tips").

❤ When you arrive at your location, make a safety check of the room. Cover electrical outlets with safety plugs, remove any dangerous objects or appliances, lock windows, and tie up long, dangling cords.

❤ If your room has a balcony, lock the doors!

❤ If you need a baby-sitter, call a bonded and licensed baby-sitting agency or check with the hotel for their recommendations. Be sure to meet the baby-sitter. When you go out, leave her the phone number of your destination and write out any instructions for taking care of your child.

Every type of transportation you use to travel with baby has its own pleasures and pitfalls. Here are some tips to maximize your enjoyment of traveling with baby.

Car

Whether your car trip is short or long, being prepared will make all the difference. Always take along your well-packed diaper bag and purse. It's a good idea to give baby a light snack and fresh diaper before you begin your trip.

Time-Tested Advice

* For long trips, pack an ice chest to hold all perishable items such as formula, dairy products, juice, fruit, baby's prepared food, and medication (should it require refrigeration).

* Age-appropriate foods to bring along are:

Birth to Six Months (Not Breast-Feeding)

⊚ A bottle or bottles of formula (depending on the length of your trip), preferably ready-to-feed for convenience, with secured cap and cover

PINK AND BLUE HINT

For the teething child, store a teething ring in the ice chest.

PINK AND BLUE ALERT

Never feed baby in a moving car! When it's time to eat, stop and feed your child. Whether the car is moving or not, remember never to feed a baby or toddler food on a stick (including lollipops and Popsicles).

PINK AND BLUE ALERT

Don't take along toys that have sharp or rough edges, protruding metal winders, or parts that can be easily swallowed and lodged in baby's throat.

PINK AND BLUE HINT

If you have time, pre-record your own tapes with baby's favorite songs and stories.

- A bottle or bottles of diluted juice with secured cap and cover

Six to Ten Months

- A bottle or bottles of formula and juice (same as birth to six months)

- Labeled, airtight containers of prepared baby food and a rubber-tipped spoon

Ten to Twenty-Four Months

- Bottles of formula or milk (after one year of age) and juice

- Labeled, airtight containers of prepared baby food and spoon or simple finger foods and snacks packed in airtight plastic bags (see Chapter 11, "Solid Food")

- Pack food for adults and older children. Don't count on baby's leftovers!

- Take a few paper bags in case of motion sickness and saltine crackers for the child who has enough teeth.

- Take a roll of paper towels for spills and general cleaning up.

- Take along an extra blanket, especially if you're traveling in cold weather.

- Dress your child for the inside car temperature. For long trips, remove your toddler's shoes (if it will make her more comfortable).

- Hang a car window shade or towel on the window next to baby to protect her from direct sunlight.

- For long excursions, stop every couple of hours to allow you and your child to stretch and get some fresh air.

- Attach a few of baby's favorite toys to the car seat so you won't have to constantly pull over to the side of the road and pick them up. No long strings or cords! Bring along enough toys to alternate during your trip to keep baby from getting bored (see Chapter 13, "Activities, Books, Music, and Toys").

- For the older toddler, don't take dolls or toys with too many accessories because they'll get lost easily.

- Take along children's musical and storytelling tapes (and, if your car doesn't have one, a portable cassette player/compact disc player with extra batteries).

- For the older toddler, an audio cassette and companion book are great entertainment.

- Take along colorful picture books with sturdy cardboard or fabric pages. Touching, smelling, and "peek-a-boo" books are great fun.

- As you drive, count with your child—a particular color car, recognizable shapes, animals, anything!

- If your child is an early toilet trainer, take along her portable toilet to continue training. Don't forget the toilet paper!

PINK AND BLUE CAR SAFETY ALERTS

- Always use the car seat for baby (see Chapter 6, "Home from the Hospital" and Chapter 12, "S.O.S.: Safety Tips").

- Everyone in the car must buckle up!

- Never let your child remain unattended in a parked car because it can be life threatening.

- Your car should be equipped with a first-aid kit at all times!

- Do not smoke in the car. Secondhand smoke is very dangerous and hazardous to baby's health.

- If your child is close to a door and window button, be certain they're locked.

- If there's an ashtray within your child's reach, be sure to close the compartment and remove the lighter.

- Carry a flashlight in your glove compartment (check the batteries often).

• Stop and feed your child when it's time to eat. If this is impossible, then make sure an adult is sitting next to the child while she eats or drinks in case she chokes.

❀ Use soft duffel bags to pack baby's clothing and toys. You can stuff more items into a bag, and it'll fit more easily in the trunk or car.

❀ When traveling long distances with toddlers, put a sheet or blanket under the baby's car seat to preserve car upholstery.

❀ Make sure your spare tire is in good shape.

PINK AND BLUE HINT

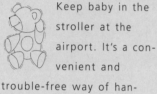

Keep baby in the stroller at the airport. It's a convenient and trouble-free way of handling your child.

Plane

When making plane travel arrangements, tell the airline or travel agent that you are traveling with a child under two years old. On domestic flights, children under two travel free, but aren't given an assigned seat or meal. If the flight isn't heavily booked, your child may occupy a seat.

PINK AND BLUE HINT

Avoid foods with too much sugar because sugar can be an energy booster for your child. The last thing children need on airplanes is more energy!

Time-Tested Advice

❀ When making reservations, request bulkhead seats. The bulkhead area of the plane has more leg space and room for your toddler to stand up and move about. Also, a bassinet, available by request from the airline, can fit in this space.

❀ If you can't reserve the bulkhead, ask for an aisle seat so you don't have to climb over other passengers and disturb them.

❀ Get your boarding passes prior to your date of departure.

- Before leaving for the airport, don't forget to call ahead and confirm your plane's departure time. If the flight is delayed, you'll save yourself unnecessary waiting time at the airport.

- Arrive at the airport a little early to deal with any unexpected complications.

- All baby equipment can be sent through as extra luggage. Label each item clearly with your name and address. There may be a charge for extra pieces. You should expect some wear and tear, though; and don't expect to be compensated for any damage.

- You can carry a baby under eighteen pounds in a soft baby carrier. Once on the plane, put the seat belt around your body, not baby's.

- You can take the car seat or infant seat on the plane with you. If the seat next to you is unoccupied, baby's seat may be strapped to the regular airplane seat. (All car seats must be FAA approved.) The airline will stow the car seat away for you if there isn't an empty seat available.

- Pre-board with baby. You can keep her in the stroller until you reach your designated seat; then fold the stroller and hang it in a nearby closet.

- On the takeoff and landing, always nurse your baby or give her a bottle or pacifier to suck on to relieve middle-ear pressure. A pacifier will also calm down an irritable, restless baby that needs to fall asleep.

PINK AND BLUE ALERT

If your child is sick or shows any signs of illness, call your pediatrician before you leave.

PINK AND BLUE HINT

Gift wrap one or two new, inexpensive toys or books for the plane ride for your toddler. It makes the flight extra special.

- In a separate bag, in addition to your diaper bag, carry along whatever you anticipate needing for your child on board and during the first twenty-four hours after your arrival. Be equipped with extra food, drink, toys, diapers, clothing, pair of pajamas, and blankets. That way, you will not need to depend on the flight attendants at all, and should your luggage arrive later than you, you'll be prepared.

- Be sure to bring your own age-appropriate food and toys on the plane for baby (see Chapter 11, "Solid Food" and Chapter 13, "Activities, Books, Music, and Toys").

- Bring extra bottled water.

- Always hold your child's hand when walking down the aisle. Don't let her run up and down the aisle and disturb other passengers.

- It's important to explain the procedures for boarding and deplaning to your toddler. She needs to understand that you're not traveling alone and there are many people on the plane. Consideration of others is imperative, particularly in a confining situation like a plane.

- It's easier and less stressful to be the last ones off the plane. This will give you the opportunity to collect all your items and change baby's diaper one last time. Plus, when you arrive at the baggage claim area, there will be less waiting time.

Train

When you travel by train, again you'll need the well-packed diaper bag and purse. If you're going on a long trip, make reservations for both you and baby. Your sanity is well worth the cost of the extra train ticket (half-price for child under two).

Time-Tested Advice

❤ Request the nonsmoking section of the train.

❤ For a baby under eighteen pounds, wear a soft baby carrier.

❤ Board early to get the seat of your choice. A window seat will be fun for your child. An aisle seat will be better for you.

❤ If there are four-seater compartments on the train, reserve one. It's a comfortable way to travel with the family.

❤ If your train ride is overnight, reserve a separate sleeping compartment if possible.

❤ In a separate bag, carry whatever you anticipate needing during your train travel, such as extra clothing, diapers, pajamas, and extra bottles.

❤ Bring along a good selection of age-appropriate toys and books to amuse your child during the train ride (see Chapter 12, "Activities, Books, Music, and Toys").

❤ Pack enough of baby's food to last the length of your train ride just as you would for a car trip.

PINK AND BLUE HINT

A small ice chest can keep formula, juices, baby's food, and other perishables from spoiling.

PINK AND BLUE TRAIN SAFETY ALERTS

• Never leave your child alone with someone you don't know well. If people offer to help, let them carry your luggage, not your child!

• Always carry your child when walking from one train car to another.

• Trains do not have seat belts, so keep a watchful eye on your child at all times.

PINK AND BLUE HINT
Prior to traveling, consult your pediatrician regarding dosages of all medications, including over-the-counter items.

Don't forget the extra bibs and baby spoon (see Chapter 11, "Solid Food").

❤ To avoid long lines for food on the train, pack your own food.

❤ Before leaving home, check to make sure the train is departing on time.

Travel Abroad: Special Guidelines

If you're planning a trip abroad, baby needs a passport just as you do. On international flights, a child under two requires a ticket at 10% the cost of an adult fare. This entitles the child to board the plane but doesn't guarantee her a separate seat. If the flight isn't heavily booked, she may occupy a seat.

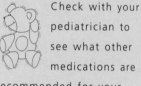

PINK AND BLUE HINT
Check with your pediatrician to see what other medications are recommended for your international trip.

Time-Tested Advice

❤ For long overseas flights, besides following the usual guidelines for plane trips and other long trips, try taking a night flight when baby would normally be sleeping. (Remember, when you arrive at your destination, try to adjust to that country's time immediately!)

❤ To be on the safe side, pack a medical kit for you and baby. Include the following:

⊚ Any prescribed medications for you and baby

⊚ Liquid antidiarrheal agents

- Liquid antihistamine

- Infant acetaminophen drops

- Liquid decongestant

- Nasal aspirator and nasal saline solution

- Ear drops

- Antibiotics for you and baby (consult your doctor and your pediatrician)

- Know your child's weight in kilos (22 kilos equal one pound). If you need a different medication, it's helpful to know baby's exact weight for correct dosage.

- Be sure your child's immunizations are current. Do this well in advance of departure. Depending on the country you're visiting, baby may require additional immunizations.

- In each city you visit, check with the American consulate for the closest recommended hospital and doctor.

- It's advisable to drink only bottled water. Wash all baby bottles and accessories in bottled water.

- Take along a box of baby's laundry detergent.

A Final Word

Parenting is the most rewarding and challenging experience you will ever have. Enjoy it! Keep a positive perspective and a sense of humor. We created this book to minimize your concerns and maximize your confidence. Trust your instincts; they will not fail you.

Index